MICROECONOMIC THEORY OLD AND NEW

MICROECONOMIC THEORY
OLD AND NEW

A Student's Guide

JOHN M. GOWDY

STANFORD ECONOMICS AND FINANCE

An Imprint of Stanford University Press
Stanford, California

Stanford University Press
Stanford, California

We are grateful to Liz Blum for preparing the illustrations included in this volume.

Printed in the United States of America on acid-free, archival-quality paper

Library of Congress Cataloging-in-Publication Data
Gowdy, John M.
    Microeconomic theory old and new : a student's guide / John M. Gowdy.
      p. cm.
    Includes bibliographical references and index.
    ISBN 978-0-8047-5883-3 (cloth : alk. paper)—ISBN 978-0-8047-5884-0
(pbk. : alk. paper)
      1. Microeconomics.   2. Equilibrium (Economics)   3. Welfare economics.
  I. Title.
HB172.G644   2010
338.5—dc22   2009011624

Typeset by Westchester Book Group

To Linda

CONTENTS

List of Figures   ix

List of Sketches   xi

Acknowledgments   xiii

PART ONE   **THE WALRASIAN SYSTEM**

Chapter 1   The Neoclassical Theory of the Consumer   5

Chapter 2   The Neoclassical Theory of Production   24

Chapter 3   General Equilibrium in a Barter Economy   42

Chapter 4   Introducing Prices: Perfect Competition and
              Pareto Efficiency   57

Chapter 5   Market Failure and the Second Fundamental
              Theorem of Welfare Economics   79

PART TWO   **MODERN WELFARE ECONOMICS**

Chapter 6   The Theoretical Critique of
              Walrasian Welfare Economics   101

Chapter 7   The Behavioral Critique of Walrasian
              Welfare Economics   120

Chapter 8   **Cost-Benefit Analysis Old and New**   143

Chapter 9   **The Future of Economic Theory and Policy**   163

Index   183

FIGURES

1.1	An indifference curve	9
1.2	Exchange as depicted in an Edgeworth box diagram	11
1.3	A contract curve showing all Pareto-efficient possibilities	14
1.4	Discounting in an Edgeworth box diagram	21
2.1	An isoquant	26
2.2	Exchange of inputs as depicted in an Edgeworth box diagram	27
2.3	A linear production function	31
2.4	A Leontief or fixed proportions production function	32
2.5	A Cobb–Douglass production function	33
2.6	Separating assembly of a bicycle into discrete technologies	38
2.7	A production function in terms of growth rates	39
3.1	From commodity consumption to utility possibilities	44
3.2	From input allocation to production	45
3.3	From the production possibilities frontier to the grand utility possibilities frontier	45
3.4	Social welfare functions	47
3.5	General equilibrium in a pure exchange economy	49
3.6	A potential Pareto improvement	52
3.7	Brouwer's fixed-point theorem	54

4.1   Maximizing utility subject to a budget constraint   59

4.2   Marginal costs and the production possibilities frontier   61

4.3   Industries and firms in a competitive market   62

4.4   Long-run competitive equilibrium   64

4.5   Factor demand in a competitive market   66

4.6   The value of the marginal product rule   67

4.7   Maximizing output subject to a cost constraint   67

4.8   A corner solution   73

4.9   Minimizing costs subject to an output constraint   74

5.1   Assumptions of the Walrasian model   80

5.2   An externality in production   81

5.3   Price and quantity of a good associated with
       a negative externality   82

5.4   The optimal provision of a public good   85

5.5   Price, output, and average cost under monopoly   86

5.6   The loss of social welfare under monopoly   87

5.7   Demand according to Hicks and Marshall   91

5.8   Income and substitution effects for a price increase
       in a normal good   91

5.9   Consumer surplus according to Hicks and Marshall   93

6.1   The cycling paradox (adapted from Varian 1992, 406)   105

6.2   A production possibilities frontier with two social welfare optima   106

6.3   Expansion paths for homothetic utility functions   108

6.4   Efficiency and social welfare: Efficiency trumps equity   110

7.1   The Prisoner's Dilemma   122

7.2   Preference filtering in the Walrasian model   136

8.1   Weak sustainability   151

8.2   Cost-benefit analysis in time and space   158

9.1   Walrasian theory depicts a self-contained system sealed
       off from nature and society   164

9.2   The economy as an evolving thermodynamic system   166

SKETCHES

1	Identical producers and consumers	1
2	Music truck	6
3	Consumers trading	7
4	Producers trading	25
5	Producers and consumers together	43
6	Professors around a blackboard	53
7	Invisible hand	58
8	Tragedy of the commons	84
9	Monopoly octopus	87
10	Walrus and butterfly	97
11	Rich taking money	102
12	The Prisoner's Dilemma	123
13	Economic man calculating	146
14	Tidal wave engulfing economist	154

ACKNOWLEDGMENTS

The concepts presented in this book represent the work of thousands of economists, mathematicians, political scientists, psychologists, philosophers, and those of many other disciplines over the last 300 years or more. In spite of its many limitations, the Walrasian model of general equilibrium in a competitive economy remains one the most impressive intellectual achievements of the twentieth century. Contemporary economists, whatever their political or philosophical orientation, must in one way or another come to grips with that model.

I was able to begin my journey as an economist thanks to the generosity of the West Virginia University Foundation. A WVU Foundation Fellowship and the GI Bill enabled me to devote the necessary time and energy to focus on my studies. While at West Virginia University, I had the good fortune to study under three professors in particular who showed me the intellectual joy of studying economics: Nicholas Georgescu-Roegen, William Miernyk, and Walter Page.

Among the many people I have had the good fortune to work with over the years, I would like to single out a few who have taught me the most over the past two decades: Jon Erickson, Charles Hall, Kozo Mayumi, Carl McDaniel, Jack Miller, Sabine O'Hara, and Jeroen van den Bergh.

MICROECONOMIC THEORY OLD AND NEW

PART ONE

THE WALRASIAN SYSTEM

INTRODUCTION AND OVERVIEW

The umbrella covering the various pieces of economic theory is called *welfare economics*. It provides the basic framework for applying the tools of economics to problems such as estimating the benefits of trade, valuing environmental features, and determining the criteria for sustainability. Far from being an esoteric footnote to economic theory, welfare economics provides the basic worldview of economists, giving answers to fundamental questions regarding the ultimate purpose of economic activity and the best policies to promote human well-being. The validity of some of the most widely used tools of economics—cost-benefit analysis, measures of total factor productivity, and Pareto efficiency—depends critically on the validity of the underlying welfare economic model.

For more than half a century, economic theory and policy has been dominated by a type of welfare economics called *Walrasian* economics, named after the political economist Léon Walras (1834–1910). The cornerstone of the Walrasian system is the characterization of human behavior embodied in "economic man," or *Homo economicus*, whose preferences are assumed to be stable, consistent, and independent of the preferences of others. With this starting point, the leading figures in the "marginalist revolution" of the 1870s— William Stanley Jevons, Vilfredo Pareto, and Walras—constructed a mathematical model of an economy in equilibrium that defined the science of economics as "the optimal allocation of scarce resources among alternative ends." In the decades following World War II this model not only came to dominate microeconomic analysis but also became the starting point for macroeconomics—the so-called microfoundations approach.

The starting point of the Walrasian system is the exchange of a fixed collection of goods among individuals bargaining directly with one another. The end result of free and voluntary exchange is that no further trading will make one person better off without making someone else worse off. This result is called *Pareto efficiency*, and it establishes one of the key ideas in modern economics, namely, the welfare benefits of trade. The next step is to introduce prices into the basic model and show that a perfectly operating market economy will duplicate the results of face-to-face bartering. The last part of the puzzle is to recognize that prices may be "imperfect" but that it is possible for enlightened intervention to correct these *market failures* and reestablish the conditions for Pareto efficiency.

THE THREE BUILDING BLOCKS OF THE WALRASIAN SYSTEM

The first building block of the Walrasian system is to establish that the free exchange of commodities will lead to Pareto efficiency in a pure barter economy. Individuals with a predetermined amount of commodities are allowed to directly and freely trade valuable goods with each other, and Pareto efficiency is achieved when no further trading can increase the well-being of one person without decreasing the well-being of another. The second building block is the demonstration that if market prices correctly reflect individual preferences, then a perfectly competitive market economy will lead to Pareto efficiency (the First Fundamental Theorem of Welfare Economics). That is, competition in free markets will exactly duplicate the Pareto efficient outcome that would result from direct negotiations and exchange in a barter economy. The third and final piece of the system is the recognition that the prices of market goods may be distorted for a variety of reasons. These price distortions, called market failures, include the broad categories of externalities, market power, and public goods. In these cases, governments have a legitimate role to play in correcting the failures of markets in order to establish the proper value (price) of things such as environmental services (the Second Fundamental Theorem of Welfare Economics). The underlying assumption is that people rationally and consistently respond to price signals.

To summarize the Walrasian system:

1. Trading in a barter economy—Unfettered bartering by agents with stable preferences will lead to Pareto efficiency, a situation in which no further trading can make one person better off without making another person worse off.

2. Adding prices—If prices correctly reflect consumer preferences, then competitive markets are always Pareto efficient. Free markets will exactly duplicate the results of a direct barter system.

3. Adjusting prices—When market failures are present, enlightened government intervention can adjust market prices so that a socially efficient Pareto outcome can be established.

These three building blocks provide the worldview of most economists. The ultimate source of value and the ultimate arbiter of efficiency in the Walrasian system are the preferences of *Homo economicus*, whatever these preferences might be and however they are formed. These building blocks hold together only if all the assumptions defining *Homo economicus* and perfect competition are met.

Today, welfare economics is undergoing a revolution that promises to fundamentally change the way economists see the world. Walrasian welfare economics is being challenged by a new economics, grounded in behavioral science, that recognizes the social and biological context of decision making and the complexity of human behavior. The current sea change in economic theory offers a unique opportunity for economists, working together with other behavioral scientists, to move mainstream economic theories and policies toward an empirical, science-based approach unbounded by a priori assumptions.

This book has two goals. The first is to present clearly and precisely how the internal logic of the Walrasian model works. What is the starting point for the model, how do the pieces fit together, and what are the policy implications? The second is to present the current revolution in welfare economics and the theoretical and empirical challenges to Walrasian theory.

FURTHER READING

An essential source for background on economics concepts, definitions, and the history of economic thought is *The New Palgrave Dictionary of Economics*, 4 vols., ed. J. Eatwell, M. Milgate, and P. Newman (London and New York: Macmillan, 1987).

Recent Microeconomic Texts

Cowell, F. 2005. *Microeconomics: Principles and Analysis*. Oxford: Oxford University Press.

Mas-Colell, A., M. Whinston, and J. Green. 1995. *Microeconomic Theory*. New York: Oxford University Press.

Varian, H. 1992. *Microeconomic Analysis*. New York: W. W. Norton.

Not-So-Recent (but Very Useful) Microeconomic Texts

Ferguson, C. E. 1969. *Microeconomic Theory*, 2nd ed. Homewood, IL: Richard Irwin.

Ferguson, C. E. 1975. *The Neoclassical Theory of Production and Distribution*. Cambridge: Cambridge University Press.

Henderson, J., and R. Quandt. 1980. *Microeconomic Theory: A Mathematical Introduction*. New York: McGraw-Hill.

Quirk, J., and R. Saposnik. 1968. *Introduction to General Equilibrium Theory and Welfare Economics*. New York: McGraw-Hill.

Silberberg, E. 1978. *The Structure of Economics: A Mathematical Analysis*. New York: McGraw-Hill.

Classic Texts

Pareto, V. [1906] 1971. *Manual of Political Economy*. New York: Augustus Kelley.

Samuelson, P. A. 1947. *Foundations of Economic Analysis*. Cambridge, MA: Harvard University Press.

Walras, L. [1926] 1977. *Elements of Pure Economics*. Fairfield, CT: Augustus Kelley.

1

THE NEOCLASSICAL THEORY
OF THE CONSUMER

> Let us return to the state of nature and consider men as if . . . sprung
> out of the earth, and suddenly, like mushrooms, come to full
> maturity without any kind of engagement to each other.
> —*Thomas Hobbes*, De Cive; or, The Citizen *[1651], edited with an*
> *introduction by Sterling P. Lamprecht (New York: Appleton-Century-*
> *Crofts, 1949), 100*

THE FOUNDATION OF UTILITY THEORY—DIRECT
EXCHANGE IN A PURE BARTER ECONOMY

Imagine you are driving along a highway behind a truck loaded with merchandise. A box falls out and lands on the side of the road and you stop to take a look and examine the contents. The box is full of CDs (compact discs) of all sorts—classical music, country and western, hip-hop, jazz, Hawaiian, and blues. There is nothing in the box to indicate ownership—no invoice, no name on the box—and you did not notice the name on the truck. You are on your way to your economics class and, feeling slightly guilty about taking the box, you decide to distribute the CDs to your classmates. Suppose there are twenty people in your class and you have 500 CDs to hand out. You start handing them out randomly, not necessarily evenly—some people end up with lots of CDs and some with only two or three. So now there is a group of twenty people sitting around a table with 500 CDs randomly distributed and unevenly divided among them. This sets the stage for learning about how economists think about prices, markets, free trade, social welfare, **utility**, and efficiency.

The Exchange of Goods in a Pure Barter Economy

The three starting points for the analysis that follows are:

1. The number of CDs to trade (500) is fixed before trading starts.

2. The distribution of these CDs among the twenty people is given before trading starts.

3. The (musical) preferences of the twenty individuals do not change during the bargaining process.

Now the fun begins. Your economics teacher seizes the opportunity to teach the class about market exchange and devotes the class time to establishing a "market equilibrium." Your fellow students start trading CDs—Brittney Spears for Bad Religion, Shostakovich for Metallica, or Green Day for Dale Watson. Trading goes on for most of the class as people haggle, barter, trade, and retrade to get the CDs they want. After an hour or so, things get quiet as no one is willing to make another deal. The students have done the best they can, *given their different musical preferences and their initial endowment of CDs.* This situation is called **Pareto efficiency,** an essential concept in neoclassical **welfare economics**.

Pareto Efficiency in the Exchange of Goods—*A situation in which no further trading of goods can make one person better off without making another person worse off.*

The process of haggling and bartering in trade is what Adam Smith had in mind when he talked about the "invisible hand" of the market economy; that is, the push-and-shove, give-and-take, dynamic vitality of capitalism. Direct bartering allows for face-to-face interaction and for nonpecuniary motives such as altruism and envy, and of course old-fashioned greed. Perhaps you refuse to trade with some people because you resent the fact that they have more CDs than you do and you do not want them to be better off than they already are. Maybe you trade five CDs with someone for one CD you do not particularly want because you are trying to get a date with him or her. All these factors may affect the "well-being" you get from the CDs and they can be incorporated into your trading decisions.

Those of you who have learned the economic model of "perfect competition" (discussed in detail in Chapter 4) might recognize that some of the conditions of that model are fulfilled in this simple barter case. For example:

perfect information—everyone knows exactly how many CDs everyone else has and who the artists are

perfect resource mobility—trade can take place almost instantaneously and at negligible cost

homogeneous product—among the CDs there might be four brand-new, identical copies of Pink Floyd's *Evolution* CD

This simple example illustrates some of the most basic ideas that economists dearly cling to.

Trade is good. All trade is assumed to be voluntary, so why would people trade if it did not make them better off?

Restrictions on trade are bad. What if the instructor limited trades to two per person? Or collected a tax for each Radiohead CD traded? This would hinder or even prevent the achievement of Pareto efficiency.

The simple model of exchange in a barter economy is in the back of most economists' minds as they make policy recommendations on everything from international trade to global warming. A question to keep in mind is: How closely does this face-to-face barter situation resemble a modern market economy with prices, distant markets, complex social institutions, and limited information?

A GRAPHICAL ANALYSIS OF BARTER AND TRADE

As useful as the verbal description of exchange is, it has limitations in terms of its analytical power. Economists deal with data about economic activity, and to interpret this data it is necessary to examine it in an analytical, meaning mathematical, framework. By adding a few more assumptions to the barter model we can reexamine our exchange example using graphs, then mathematics.

One of the most basic and critical tools of Walrasian analysis is the **indifference curve,** as depicted in Figure 1.1. The points on a particular indifference curve show all the combinations of two commodities (X and Y in Figure 1.1)

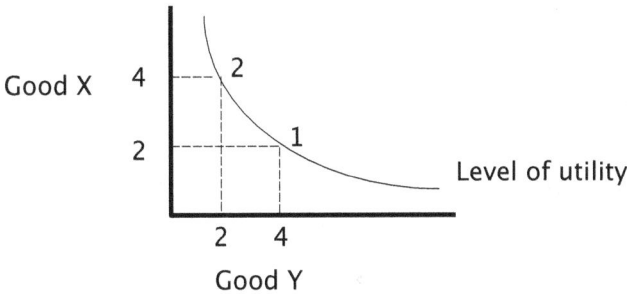

Figure 1.1. An indifference curve

that yield the same level of utility. In fact, it might be called an iso-utility curve, analogous to isothermals on a weather map. According to Figure 1.1, the consumer is just as happy with the combination of goods X and Y given by point 1 as he or she is with the combination given by point 2. The consumer is just as happy with 2X and 4Y as he or she is with 4X and 2Y.

The indifference curve in Figure 1.1 embodies a number of assumptions about human behavior. The economic analysis of consumer behavior is based on a conception of human nature defined by the assumptions of *Homo economicus*, or "economic man" (sometimes called the rational actor model). Economic man has well-defined preferences that are stable over time. Individual welfare (utility) is equated with the consumption of market commodities, as shown by the axes of the diagram—goods X and Y. More is preferred to less, so higher indifference curves, those farther away from the origin, represent more total utility to the consumer than ones closer to the origin. Commodities are subject to substitution, as indicated by the downward slope of the indifference curve. Indifference curves have the mathematical property of being "smooth and continuous," meaning there are no "jumps" in utility as one commodity is substituted for another as we move along the curve.

Axioms of Consumer Choice Defining *Homo economicus* (*economic* man or the *rational actor*)

1. Non-satiation—More is preferred to less. A commodity bundle on a higher indifference curve is preferred to one on a lower indifference curve.

2. Transitivity—If commodity bundle A is preferred to bundle B, and bundle B is preferred to C, then bundle A is preferred to C. This implies consistency in consumer choice.

3. Preferences are stable and complete—For any pair of commodity bundles A and B, the consumer either prefers A to B, B to A, or is indifferent between the two bundles. These preferences are stable over time.

4. Diminishing marginal rates of substitution—As a consumer has more of one commodity relative to another one, he/she is willing to give up more of it for a unit of the second commodity.

5. Continuity—This is a mathematical property, meaning that any point on a line drawn between two points on an indifference curve is an *interior point*. As we will see later, this assumption is necessary to ensure a unique solution to any *constrained maximization* problem.

6. Exogenous preferences—The preferences of one consumer are unaffected by the preferences of others.

The slope of an indifference curve at a particular place along a curve, $\Delta X / \Delta Y$ or the "rise over the run," indicates the **marginal rate of substitution** (MRS) of one commodity for another. For example, as we go between points 1 and 2, the marginal rate of substitution of good Y for good X ($MRS_{Y\ for\ X}$) is -1, $\Delta X / \Delta Y = -2/2 = -1$. The consumer is willing to give up 1 X to get 1 Y without changing total utility. The shape of the curves, becoming steeper or flatter as they approach the X or Y axes, indicates a *diminishing marginal rate of substitution*. As a consumer has more and more of good X (or good Y), he or she is willing to give up more and more of X (or Y) to get another Y (or X).

It is important to recognize the assumptions invoked in the basic model of exchange in a barter situation and those that are added as we move from a verbal to a graphical and then to a mathematical representation of exchange. Remember that this model is meant to be a plausible representation of actual human behavior. When we move to a graphical representation of utility, what assumptions are added to the three we started with in the pure barter case?

▶ **ASSUMPTION ALERT!** *Critical behavioral assumptions we have added to move from a verbal to a graphical analysis of exchange:*

1. *The utility of one individual can be determined independently of the utility of others.*

2. *Utility or well-being is equated with consumption of the market goods X and Y.*

3. *More consumption is always preferred to less.*

4. *All items giving an individual "utility" are subject to substitution and trade.* ◀

FROM INDIFFERENCE CURVES TO EXCHANGE:
THE EDGEWORTH BOX DIAGRAM

Armed with our model of human behavior and our goal of efficiency, we can develop a set of rules about how two people (or more than two people using mathematics) will engage in barter and trade to make themselves better off. The diagram in Figure 1.2 is called an *Edgeworth box*, named after the economist and mathematician Francis Edgeworth (1845–1926).

Figure 1.2 is actually two indifference curve diagrams put together, one for consumer A and one for consumer B. The origin for consumer A is at the

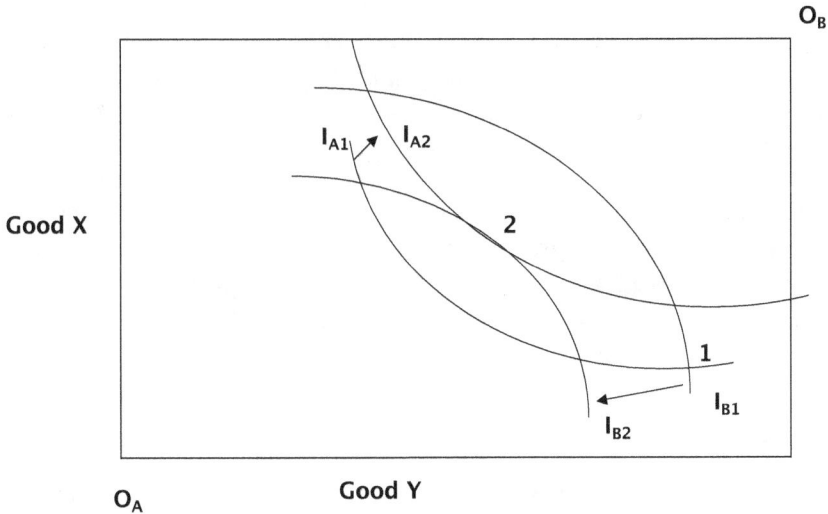

Figure 1.2. Exchange as depicted in an Edgeworth box diagram

lower left-hand corner so that his utility increases steadily as we move up and to the right in the Edgeworth box (because he has more of goods A and B). The origin for consumer B is at the upper right-hand corner so that her utility increases as we move down and to the left in the Edgeworth box. Any point inside the Edgeworth box shows the distribution of the two goods among the two consumers.

Notice that if we move from point 1 to point 2, the utility for both consumers increases. Consumer A moves from indifference curve I_{A1} to the higher indifference curve I_{A2} and consumer B moves from indifference curve I_{B1} to the higher indifference curve (farther from the origin for B) I_{B2}. At point 2 both consumers have been made better off by trading. A movement from point 1 to point 2 in Figure 1.2 is a graphical representation of a voluntary trade of one CD for another in the barter example we began with.

Notice that at point 2 no further trading can take place without making one of the consumers worse off. If we move away from point 2 to anywhere else on indifference curve I_{A2}, consumer B moves to an indifference curve with less utility. If we move from point 2 to any other point on indifference curve I_{B2}, consumer A is on a lower indifference curve with less total utility. Point 2 is a Pareto-efficient point. Now looking at the indifference curves for the two consumers at point 2 we can see something very important. The indifference curves are just tangent to one another, indicating that their slopes (their marginal rates of substitution of X for Y) are the same.

Pareto Condition I. *The condition for Pareto efficiency in exchange in a barter economy is that the marginal rates of substitution between the two goods is the same for the two consumers. When this occurs, no further trading can increase the utility of one consumer without decreasing the utility of the other.*

▶ ASSUMPTION ALERT!

1. *This is a model of the static exchange of a fixed amount of goods among consumers with stable preferences, and each consumer has (implicitly) perfect information about the characteristics of the goods and the preferences of the other consumer.*

2. *The particular Pareto-efficient outcome depends on the initial distribution of the goods among the two consumers. Look at Figure 1.2 and convince yourself that a different initial distribution of X and Y will result in a different Pareto-efficient distribution.* ◄

CRITICAL THINKING—The rationale for the benefits of exchange depicted in Figure 1.2 is perhaps the single most important concept in contemporary economic theory and policy. Answer the following questions based on Figure 1.2 and then critically examine your answers in light of the assumptions underlying the figure. Think of real-world examples and real-world complications.

1. Why do most economists advocate free trade?

2. Why do most economists insist that the optimal amount of pollution is greater than zero?

3. So far we have said nothing about prices; all trade is the result of direct negotiations. How would using prices as indicators of value change your answers to questions 1 and 2?

REMEMBER, THINK CRITICALLY!

ONE MORE THING BEFORE MOVING ON—
THE MANY PARETO EFFICIENCIES

For any particular initial distribution of goods X and Y among consumers A and B, there will be only one Pareto-efficient outcome of trade. Each different initial distribution of X and Y will yield a different Pareto-efficient outcome. A line connecting all the Pareto points in an Edgeworth box is called a **contract curve**, and such a curve is shown in Figure 1.3. We will return to the contract curve later when we discuss the notion of a **social welfare function**. Given the preferences of the two consumers A and B, for the two goods X and Y, as depicted by the shapes of the indifference curves, the contract curve shows the Pareto-efficient allocations of the two goods *for all possible* initial distributions of the two goods between the two consumers.

Figure 1.3 illustrates a very important concept lying at the base of Walrasian economic policy. By altering the initial distribution of goods X and Y (this is called a **lump-sum transfer**), any particular Pareto-efficient outcome

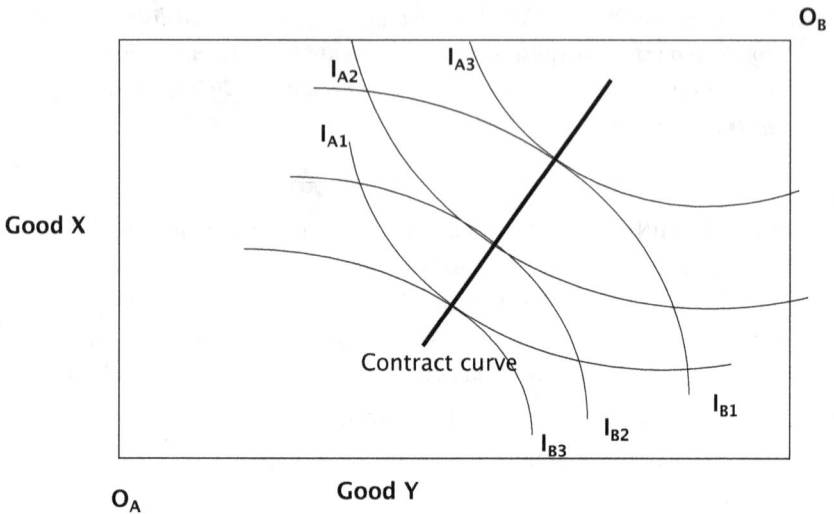

Figure 1.3. A contract curve showing all Pareto-efficient possibilities

can be reached. This has important implications for economic policy. In this framework the ideal policy to correct inequality, for example, is to let the political process set the parameters (the initial distribution of goods) and let the "market" determine the final outcome. This preserves the efficiency of the trading process.

THE MATHEMATICAL INTERPRETATION OF UTILITY

Mathematically, the indifference curve may be stated as a **utility function** of the form:

(1.1) $U_A = f(X,Y)$

The utility of consumer A is a function of (depends on) the amounts of commodities X and Y consumed. Much of Walrasian analysis uses the mathematics of **constrained optimization**. This mathematics is very simple but it can be intimidating to the uninitiated. Most of the mathematics in economics deals with marginal change, which is expressed by the concept of the derivative. For example, the change in utility of consumer A that results from a change in the amount of good X is expressed as dU / dX (or using the Greek letter delta, $\Delta U / \Delta X$ or $\partial U / \partial X$). It shows the effect of a small change in the amount of good X on total utility *with the amounts of all other goods possessed by consumer A held constant.* This is called the **marginal utility** of X. Likewise, dU / dY is the marginal utility of good Y.

Referring to equation (1.1), we can perform a mathematical operation called total differentiation to examine the change in utility resulting from changes in the amounts of goods X and Y.

(1.2) $dU = (dU / dX)\,\Delta X + (dU / dY)\,\Delta Y$

The change in total utility in the simple two-good economy is equal to the marginal utility of X, that is, how a one-unit change in X (or dX) changes the utility of the consumer (or dU), multiplied by the actual unit change in X (or ΔX) plus the marginal utility of Y multiplied by the actual unit change in Y. For example, if the marginal utility of X is 2 "utils" and the marginal utility of Y is 3 "utils," and we give the consumer 2 more X's and 3 more Y's, the consumer's utility goes up by $2 \cdot 2 + 3 \cdot 3 = 13$ utils.

By definition, utility does not change along an indifference curve, so $dU = 0$. Thus we can rewrite equation (1.2) as:

(1.3) $(dU / dX)\,\Delta X = -(dU / dY)\,\Delta Y$ or

(1.4) $(dX / dY) = -(dU / dY) / (dU / dX) = -(MU_Y / MU_X) = MRS_{Y\,for\,X}$

Along an indifference curve, the ratio of marginal utilities is equal to the (negative) slope of the indifference curve, (dX / dY). So the slope of the indifference curve at any particular point shows the rate at which the consumer can substitute one good for another and keep her utility constant. Stated another way, the ratio of marginal utilities of the two goods is equal to the marginal rate of substitution of one of those goods for the other.

Terms and Concepts to Know Before Moving On (see the glossary at the end of the chapter)

Diminishing marginal rate of substitution

Exogenous preferences

Homo economicus

Indifference curve

Marginal rate of substitution

Marginal utility

Pareto efficiency in exchange

Utility

Utility function

Welfare economics

CONSTRAINED OPTIMIZATION

Economic analysis is dominated by models of constrained optimization. Models are constructed to maximize one thing (utility, production, profit) subject to some constraint (income, production costs). The mathematics may seem complicated at first blush, but once you learn the principle of constrained optimization you can apply it to a wide variety of economic problems.

The CD trading example is a constrained optimization problem. Each person playing the game attempts to maximize the satisfaction gained from his or her collection of CDs given the following initial constraints:

1. The total collection of CDs to be traded is given.
2. The initial distribution of these CDs among consumers is given.
3. The preferences of all participants are consistent and stable.

By trading with each other, consumers A and B maximize the utility they derive from consuming goods X and Y given the three initial conditions. They trade goods until they reach a point where any further trading would make at least one of them worse off. At this point the slopes of the indifference curves of the two consumers are the same, which means that the marginal rates of substitution of good X for good Y is the same for both consumers.

Mathematically, the constrained optimization problem looks like this:

$$(1.5) \qquad Z_A = U_A(X_A, Y_A) + \lambda[U_B(X^0 - X_A, Y^0 - Y_A) - U_B^0]$$

Equation (1.5) is called a *Lagrangian* equation and is an indispensable tool of Walrasian welfare economics. By convention, we use Z for the Lagrange equation rather than L so as not to confuse it with equations for labor. The utility of consumer A (U_A) is maximized subject to the available amounts of the goods—total amounts of the goods minus those consumed by consumer B. The total amounts of the two goods are given as $X^0 = X_A + X_B$ and $Y^0 = Y_A + Y_B$. λ is the *Lagrangian multiplier*, and it is discussed in more detail in Chapter 4.

The combination of goods X and Y that give the highest possible utility to consumer A can be found by taking the partial derivatives (denoted by Δ) of Z_A with respect to X_A, Y_A, and λ.

(1.6) $\partial Z_A / \partial X_A = \partial U_A / \partial X_A - \lambda(\partial U_B / \partial X_B) = 0$

(1.7) $\partial Z_A / \partial Y_A = \partial U_A / \partial Y_A - \lambda(\partial U_B / \partial Y_B) = 0$

(1.8) $\partial Z_A / \partial \lambda = U_B(X^0 - X_A, Y^0 - Y_A) - U_B^0$

Dividing equation (1.6) by equation (1.7) yields the condition for maximizing the utility of consumer A, given the fixed utility of consumer B:

(1.9) $(\partial U_A / \partial X_A) / (\partial U_A / \partial Y_A) = (\partial U_B / \partial X_B) / (\partial U_B / \partial Y_B)$

This is exactly the same condition for Pareto efficiency that we saw earlier in Figure 1.2. The ratios of the marginal utilities of goods X and Y (the marginal rates of substitution) have to be the same for both consumers A and B. When this condition is fulfilled, no further trading of the goods can make one person better off without making the other person worse off.

THE NECESSITY OF THE INDEPENDENT UTILITIES ASSUMPTION IN WALRASIAN THEORY

Notice that the utility function for consumer A (equation [1.5]) does not depend directly on the utility of consumer B but only on the amounts of X and Y he consumes. His utility is unaffected by the amounts of X and Y that consumer B has. The assumption of independent utilities is critical to the result shown in equation (1.9). To ensure Pareto efficiency, the rates of commodity substitution, Y for X, have to be the same for both consumers. As Chapter 3 shows, this result is critical for establishing the conditions for general equilibrium in a competitive economy. If the consumption of one consumer is directly affected by the level of utility of the other consumer, as in the utility functions,

(1.10) $U_A = U_A(X_A, Y_A, X_B, Y_B)$ and $U_B = U_A(X_A, Y_A, X_B, Y_B)$

then the first condition for Pareto efficiency does not hold, that is, $MRS^A_{Y \text{ for } X} \neq MRS^B_{Y \text{ for } X}$, and the conditions of general equilibrium (see Chapter 3) cannot be established (for a mathematical proof of this, see Henderson and Quandt 1980, 297). Numerous experiments in the fields of behavioral economics, neuroscience, and psychology have established that preference formation is in fact "other regarding," that is, the utility of one person is affected by the utility of others. The implications of these findings for utility theory are explored in Part Two.

APPENDIX

Convexity Tests

The assumption of the convexity of indifference curves is necessary to ensure a unique solution to any consumer maximization problem. Convexity ensures that the indifference curves for the two consumers are tangent at only one point. Graphically, convexity means that all the points on a line drawn between any two points on the indifference curve are interior points. Without convexity we could have multiple tangency points between two indifference curves. We also need to establish that utility is being maximized, not minimized. If utility is at a maximum level, then any movement away from that point subtracts from total utility (a negative number).

Mathematically, convexity and utility maximization can be established by starting with the utility function:

(1.11) $U^0 = f(X, Y)$, where utility is constant at U^0.

The total differential of this function is $dU = (\partial U / \partial X)dX + (\partial U / \partial Y)dY$. The change in utility (dU) is equal to the change in utility from an additional unit of good X ($\partial U / \partial X$) times the change in the number of units of good X (dX) plus the change in utility from an additional unit of good Y ($\partial U / \partial Y$) times the change in the number of units of good Y (dY).

We are moving along an indifference curve, meaning that utility is unchanged, $dU=0$, so we can write:

(1.12) $dU=(\partial U/\partial X)dX+(\partial U/\partial Y)dY=0$, and

(1.13) $dY/dX=-(\partial U/\partial X)/(\partial U/\partial Y)$

The slope of the indifference curve (dY/dX) equals the ratio of marginal utilities of X and Y, which is the marginal rate of substitution of Y for X. Either ∂X or ∂Y must be negative to offset the positive effect of a change in the amount of the other good.

We can further differentiate equation (1.13), yielding the second differentiation of equation (1.11), to get:

(1.14) $d^2Y/dX^2=[-1/(\partial U/\partial Y)^3]\,[(\partial^2 U/\partial X^2)\,(\partial U/\partial Y)^2-2\,(\partial^2 U/\partial X\partial Y)$
$(\partial U/\partial X)(\partial U\partial Y)+(\partial^2 U/\partial Y^2)\,(\partial U/\partial X)^2]$

Equation (1.14) shows the rate of change of the slope of the indifference curve.

In order for the indifference curve to have a negative slope, the function must be differentiable (smooth and continuous) and the value of the term within the brackets of equation (1.14) must be negative:

(1.15) $(\partial^2 U/\partial X^2)\,(\partial U/\partial Y)^2-2\,(\partial^2 U/\partial X\partial Y)\,(\partial U/\partial X)\,(\partial U\partial Y)$
$+(\partial^2 U/\partial Y^2)\,(\partial U/\partial X)^2<0$

Equation (1.15) can be used to test the convexity of specific forms of the utility function. For example, consider the function $U=XY$. Does this function pass the convexity test?

$\partial U/\partial X=Y$

$\partial U/\partial Y=X$

$\partial^2 U/\partial X^2=0$

$\partial^2 U/\partial X\partial Y=1$

$\partial^2 U/\partial Y^2=0$

$\partial^2 U/\partial Y\partial X=1$

Substituting these results into equation (1.15) yields:

(1.16) $(0)(X^2) - 2(1)(Y)((X) + (0)(Y^2) + (0)(Y^2) = -2YX < 0$

This function is convex so long as positive amounts of each good are consumed.

Discounting

As we have seen, the basic Walrasian model is one of static exchange—it depicts a one-shot exchange of a fixed set of goods. In real market situations the time factor is critical. In our CD example, suppose we want to trade one CD for the promise of another to be delivered at some point in the future. We know that, in general, we would rather have something now than later, so a CD received a year from now is worth less than one received now. This difference in value is captured by a discount rate. For example, if something received a year from now is worth only 90 percent of what it is worth if received now, this implies a discount rate of 10 percent.

Using a discount rate allows us to take the time dimension into account without changing the basic framework of analysis. Referring to Figure 1.4, if good Y is delivered in the future, all we have to do is apply the discount rate r according to the discount formula $(1+r)^{-t}$ and proceed as usual.

GLOSSARY

Constrained optimization—The maximization or minimization of an objective function subject to constraints imposed on the independent variable. For example, maximizing utility subject to an income constraint or minimizing costs subject to an output constraint.

Contract curve for exchange—The locus of all Pareto-efficient points in an Edgeworth box diagram, each point representing a different initial distribution of goods. At each point on the contract curve, the marginal rates of substitution between the two goods are the same for the two consumers.

Convexity test—A mathematical determination of whether a function (a utility function in this chapter) is smooth and continuous. Convexity is neces-

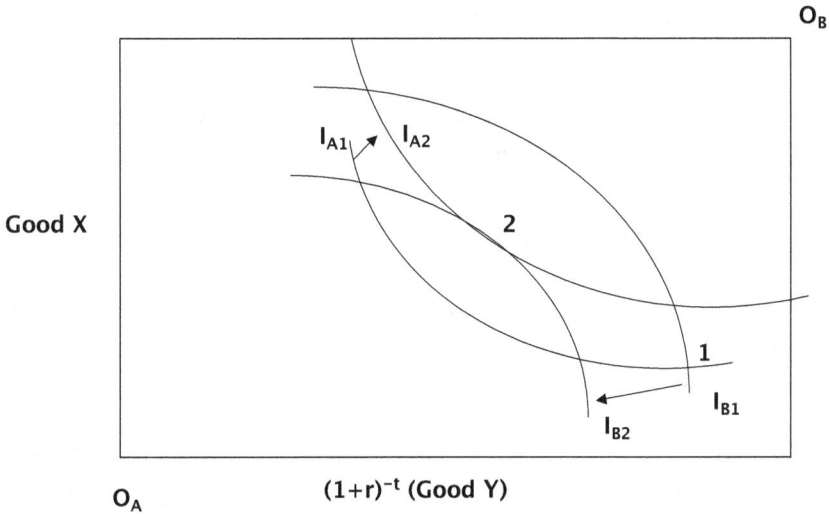

Figure 1.4. Discounting in an Edgeworth box diagram

sary to demonstrate that there exists a unique combination of goods that maximizes a consumer's utility.

Diminishing marginal rate of substitution—As the amount of one good increases relative to another good, the more of the first good a consumer is willing to give up in exchange for the second good, keeping total utility constant.

Diminishing marginal utility—As a consumer obtains more and more of one good, the amounts of all other goods held constant, the point will be reached where the utility from an additional unit begins to decline.

Discounting—The assumption is made in economic theory that a good delivered in the future is worth less than that same good delivered presently. Discounting determines how much less goods delivered in the future are worth, valued from the point of view of the present.

Exogenous preferences—Assumption that human preferences are entirely self-regarding, that is, commodity bundles are evaluated independently of what other people have or choose. Preferences can be evaluated outside (they are exogenous to) social context.

Homo economicus—Rational economic man, whose preferences are consistent, insatiable, and independent of the preferences of others.

Indifference curve—A curve showing all the combinations of two goods yielding the same amount of utility.

Lump-sum transfer—In general equilibrium analysis, the transfer of some initial endowment of goods from one person to another. Equilibrium will still be attained, but the Pareto-efficient distribution of goods will be changed.

Marginal rate of substitution—The rate at which a consumer can substitute one good for another without changing his or her level of total utility. Also called the rate of commodity substitution.

Marginal utility—The additional utility obtained from one additional unit of a commodity, the amounts of all other commodities held constant.

Pareto efficiency in exchange—In consumption, a situation in which no further trading of goods can make one person better off without making another person worse off.

Social welfare function—A graph or curve showing all the possible combinations of individual utilities where social welfare is the same. The social welfare function is based on given preferences, technology and resource endowment, and some specific ethical assumption about the fair distribution of goods among consumers.

Utility—The amount of satisfaction derived from consuming market goods and services.

Utility function—Expresses utility or well-being as a function of the quantities of market goods consumed. In this chapter, we have seen the general form $U_A = f(X,Y)$. Utility functions may also be written to indicate specific functional relationships between the commodities, such as the general Cobb–Douglas ($U = AX^aY^b$), linear ($U = aX+bY$), or fixed proportions (Leontief) ($U = \min(aX, bY)$) utility functions.

Welfare economics—The branch of economics dealing with the welfare or well-being of human society.

REFERENCE

Henderson, J., and J. Quandt. 1980. *Microeconomc Theory: A Mathematical Approach.* New York: McGraw-Hill.

2

THE NEOCLASSICAL THEORY
OF PRODUCTION

> Assuming equilibrium, we may even go so far as to abstract from
> entrepreneurs and simply consider the productive services as being,
> in a certain sense, exchanged directly for one another.
> —*Léon Walras*, Elements of Pure Economics *[1874] (London: George Allen
> and Unwin, 1954), 225*

THE FOUNDATION OF PRODUCTION THEORY—INPUT
EXCHANGE IN A BARTER ECONOMY

We saw in Chapter 1 how two consumers in a barter economy allocate their
scarce resources (the goods in their possession) in order to maximize their well-
being. The other side of the coin in a modern economy is production, and the
neoclassical analysis of production uses exactly the same framework as does
the model of consumers exchanging goods. Consumers are the locus of "consumption" and firms are the locus of "production." In the pure model of production, firms directly exchange productive inputs with other firms in order
to increase output.

In our analysis, we will assume there are only two firms that use two inputs, capital (K) and labor (L), to produce two goods, X and Y.

Input Exchange in a Pure Barter Economy

The three starting points for the analysis that follows are:

1. The inputs to be exchanged—the amounts of capital and labor—are
   given at the start of the analysis.

2. The initial distribution of the inputs among the firms is given at the
   start of the analysis.

3. Technology—the way in which capital and labor are used to produce the output of goods X and Y—does not change during the period of analysis.

Just as consumers exchanged goods so as to maximize utility, so too do firms exchange inputs so as to maximize output. Consumers have different tastes (different utility functions, in economic jargon) and firms have different technologies (different **production functions**). Firms keep trading inputs until no further trading can increase the output of one firm without decreasing the output of another firm. This is exactly the same concept of **Pareto efficiency in exchange** described in Chapter 1, only now applied to production.

> **Pareto Efficiency in Input Allocation**—*A situation in which no further trading of inputs can increase the output of one firm without decreasing the output of another firm.*

THE GRAPHICAL ANALYSIS OF INPUT ALLOCATION

The production equivalent of the indifference curve is the **isoquant**, or "same quantity," showing the different combinations of capital and labor that can be used to produce the same amount of output. Figure 2.1 shows how a firm uses

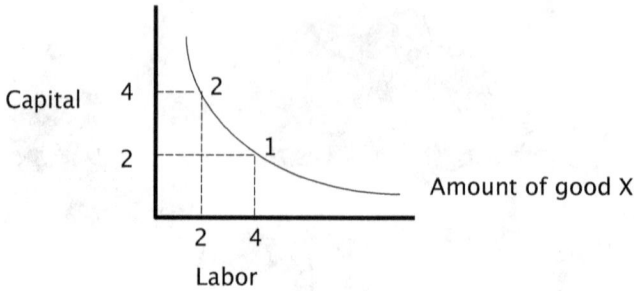

Figure 2.1. An isoquant

productive inputs, labor and capital, to produce a particular good X. The same amount of good X can be produced using either four units of capital and two units of labor or by using two units of capital and four units of labor. In the same way that commodities are subject to substitution in consumption, so too are inputs subject to substitution in production as indicated by the downward slope of the isoquant. Higher isoquants, farther away from the origin, represent more total output than ones closer to the origin. Isoquants, like indifference curves, have the mathematical property of being smooth and continuous; there are no "jumps" in output as one input is substituted for another. Keep in mind that the shape of isoquants says something about the physical nature of production. That is, when we assume smooth and continuous isoquants, we are saying that capital and labor are perfectly malleable. If we want to produce 10 units of X per day, for example, there is a machine available that is exactly the right size to do that, and a slightly larger one to produce 11 units of X, and so on.

The slope of an isoquant at a particular place along a curve, $\Delta K/\Delta L$, again the "rise over the run," indicates the **marginal rate of technical substitution** (MRTS) of one input for another. For example, between points 1 and 2 in Figure 2.1 the marginal rate of technical substitution of input K for input L (MRTS$_{L \text{ for } K}$) is 1. At that point the firm can reduce the input of K by two units and add two units of L without changing total output. The shape of the isoquants, becoming steeper or flatter as they approach the K or L axes, indicates a **diminishing marginal rate of technical substitution**. As shown in

Figure 2.1, as a firm uses more and more of input K, it takes more of input K relative to input L to keep production at the same level.

▶ **ASSUMPTION ALERT!** *Critical assumptions made so far about production:*

1. *All inputs used to produce a particular good are substitutable for one another.*

2. *Inputs are malleable, that is, there is no "lumpiness" in the production process.*

3. *The shapes of isoquants may vary, but whichever one is used is taken to be an adequate representation of the physical and technological reality of producing the good in question.* ◀

PARETO EFFICIENCY IN INPUT ALLOCATION

The trading of productive inputs among firms can also be examined using an Edgeworth box diagram. Figure 2.2 depicts the trade of two inputs (K and L) between two firms producing goods X and Y. Any point in the Edgeworth box represents the allocation of the two inputs between the two firms. Notice that if we move from point 1 to point 2 in the Edgeworth box, the production of both goods X and Y increases. The production of good X shifts from isoquant

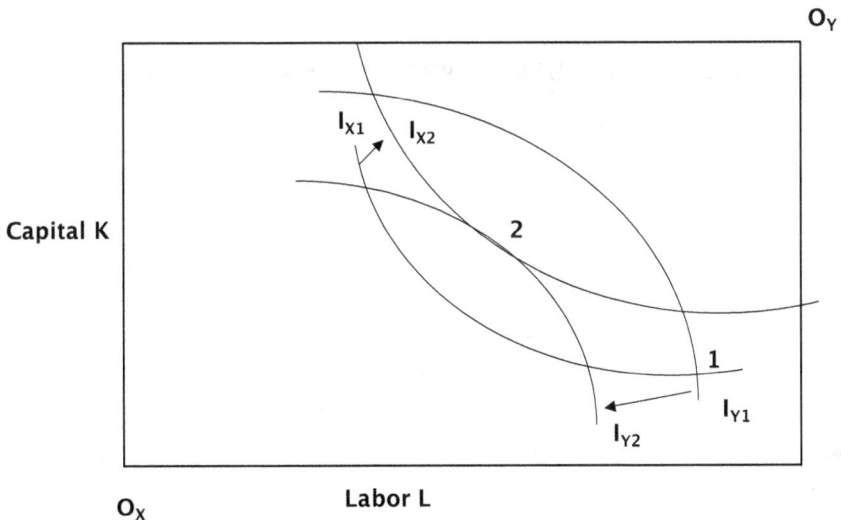

Figure 2.2. Exchange of inputs as depicted in an Edgeworth box diagram

I_{X1} to the higher isoquant I_{X2} and the production of good Y moves from isoquant I_{Y1} to the higher isoquant (farther away from the origin for Y) I_{Y2}.

Notice that at point 2 no further trading of inputs can take place without reducing the output of at least one good. If we move away from point 2 to anywhere else on isoquant I_{X2}, the production of good Y has to occur on an isoquant closer to the origin with lower output. Likewise, if we move from point 2 to any other point on isoquant I_{Y2}, the production of good X is reduced because we are on a lower isoquant with less total output. Point 2 is a *Pareto-efficient* point for the production of goods X and Y. At this point the isoquants for the production of both goods are tangent to one another indicating that their slopes are the same, that is $MRTS^X_{L\ for\ K} = MRTS^Y_{L\ for\ K}$.

> **Pareto Condition II.** *The condition for Pareto efficiency in production in a barter economy is that the marginal rates of technical substitution for the two inputs are the same for the production of both goods. When this occurs, no further trading can increase the production of one good without decreasing the production of another good.*

THE MATHEMATICAL INTERPRETATION OF THE ISOQUANT

Mathematically, the isoquant curve may be stated as a production function of the general form:

(2.1) $Q_X = f(K,L)$

The quantity of good X produced is a function of the amounts of capital and labor used. As in the problem of consumer choice discussed above, Walrasian analysis uses the mathematics of constrained optimization to describe production. The change in the output of good X resulting from a change in the amount of capital used is expressed as dQ_X/dK, $\Delta Q_X/\Delta K$ or $\partial Q_X/\partial K$. It shows the effect of a small change in the amount of K on the total output of X. This is called the **marginal product** of capital. Likewise, dQ_X/dL is the marginal product of labor.

Just as we did for the utility function in Chapter 1, we can totally differentiate the production function depicted in equation (2.1) to examine the change in output resulting from changes in the amounts of inputs K and L.

(2.2) $dQ_X = (dQ_X / dK) \Delta K + (dQ_X / dL) \Delta L$

The change in the total output of X is equal to the marginal product of capital (the effect of a one unit change in K on Q_X) multiplied by the actual unit change in K times the marginal product of L multiplied by the actual unit change in L. For example, if the marginal product of K is 2 X and the marginal product of L is 3 X, and we give the producer two more K's and three more L's, the output of X goes up by $2 \cdot 2 + 3 \cdot 3 = 13$ X.

By definition, the amount produced does not change along an isoquant, so $dQ_X = 0$. Thus we can rewrite equation (2.2) as:

(2.3) $(dQ_X / dL) \Delta L = -(dQ_X / dK) \Delta K$

Because either dL or dK must be negative along an isoquant, we can write this using positive signs as:

(2.4) $(dQ_X / dL) / (dQ_X / dK) = (MP_L / MP_K) = MRTS_{L \text{ for } K} = (dK / dL)$

Along an isoquant, the ratio of marginal products (the marginal rate of technical substitution of L for K) is equal to the (negative) slope of the isoquant, $-(dK / dL)$. So the slope of the isoquant at any particular point shows the rate at which labor can be substituted for capital and keep output constant. The marginal rate of technical substitution of one input for another is equal to the ratio of the marginal products of those inputs.

Terms and Concepts to Know Before Moving On (see the glossary at the end of the chapter)

Diminishing marginal productivity

Diminishing marginal rate of technical substitution

Isoquant

Marginal rate of technical substitution

Pareto efficiency in production

Production function

CONSTRAINED OPTIMIZATION

As in the case of consumers trading goods, the problem of firms trading inputs can also be examined using a constrained optimization approach. Each firm attempts to maximize its output by trading inputs with other firms, given the initial constraints:

1. The total amounts of inputs are given.
2. The initial distribution of these inputs between the firms is given.
3. The technology used by the firms does not change.

In Figure 2.2, firms X and Y maximize the output of the goods they produce given their technology (production functions) and initial endowment of K and L. This occurs when the slopes of the isoquants of the two firms are the same, which means that the marginal rates of technical substitution of inputs K and L are the same for both firms.

Mathematically, the constrained optimization problem looks like this:

$$(2.5) \quad Z_X = Q_X(K_X, L_X) + \mu[Q_Y(K^0 - K_A, L^0 - L_A) - Q_Y^0]$$

The output of firm $X(Q_X)$ is maximized subject to the given available amounts of the inputs—which would be the total amounts of the inputs K and L minus those used by firm Y. The total amounts of the two inputs are given as $K^0 = K_X + K_Y$ and $L^0 = L_X + L_Y$. The symbol μ is the Lagrangian multiplier.

The combination of inputs K and L yielding the highest possible output for firm X can be found by taking the partial derivatives of Q_X^* with respect to K_X, L_X, and λ.

$$(2.6) \quad \partial Z_X / \partial K_X = \partial Q_X / \partial K_X - \mu \, (\partial Q_Y / \partial L_Y) = 0$$

$$(2.7) \quad \partial Z_X / \partial L_X = \partial Q_X / \partial L_X - \mu \, (\partial Q_Y / \partial L_Y) = 0$$

$$(2.8) \quad \partial Z_X / \partial \mu = Q_Y(K^0 - K_X, L^0 - L_X) - Q_Y^0$$

Dividing equation (2.6) by equation (2.7) yields the condition for maximizing the output of firm X, given the fixed output of firm Y:

$$(2.9) \quad (\partial Q_X / \partial K_X) / (\partial Q_X / \partial L_X) = (\partial Q_Y / \partial K_Y) / (\partial Q_Y / \partial L_Y)$$

This is exactly the same condition for Pareto efficiency that we saw in Chapter 1, except now we are dealing with marginal products instead of marginal utilities. The ratios of the marginal products of inputs K and L (the marginal rates of technical substitution) have to be the same for both firms X and Y. When this condition is fulfilled, no further trading of the inputs can increase the output of one firm without decreasing the output of the other.

MORE ON PRODUCTION FUNCTIONS

The production function in equation (2.1) is written in what is called a "general form." It merely states that the production of good X depends on some amounts of the inputs K and L. In empirical studies of substitution possibilities among inputs, the production function must be given a specific mathematical form. Different forms make different assumptions about the nature of substitution among inputs, that is, about the nature of production technology. For example, a linear production function assumes that output is an additive function of the inputs used.

In the case of a linear production function (Figure 2.3), inputs are very easily substituted for one another. In fact, good X can be produced using only labor or only capital. The input substitution possibilities are infinite.

At the other end of the scale is the Leontief or fixed proportion production function (Figure 2.4), named after the economist Wassily Leontief, who received a Nobel Prize in economics for his pioneering work in input-output analysis.

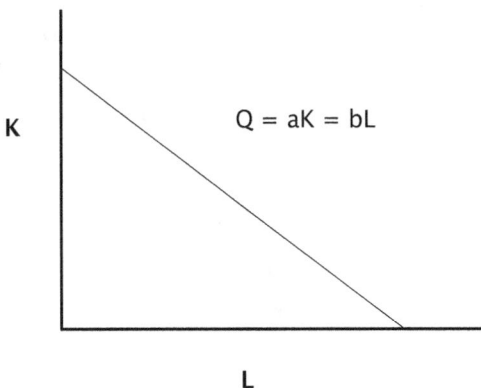

$$Q = aK = bL$$

Figure 2.3. A linear production function

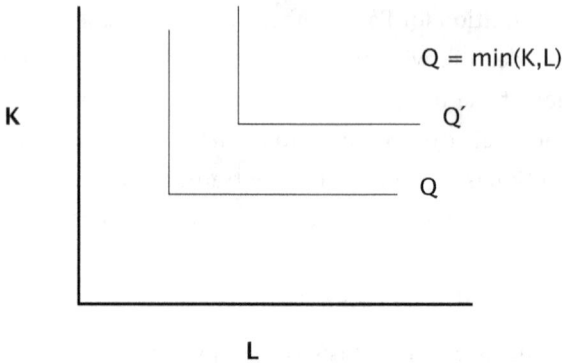

Figure 2.4. A Leontief or fixed proportions production
function

In this case there are no substitution possibilities among inputs. To produce
more output, both labor and capital are needed, and they are needed in exact
proportions. No substitution is possible among inputs.

One of the most widely used functional forms for the production function
is the Cobb–Douglas production function (Figure 2.5), proposed by Charles
Cobb and Paul Douglas in 1927 (and apparently it was used even earlier). It
describes output as a function of the inputs capital and labor and a technological parameter "A." In its simple form, technology is assumed to be *exogenous* so that a technology advance (an increase in A) will allow more output
to be produced with given amounts of capital and labor.

The shape of the Cobb–Douglas function is a rectangular hyperbola. This
implies that as the amount of one input increases relative to the amount of
the other, past a certain point the marginal product of the first input will decline. This brings up an important concept in production theory known as
the **elasticity of substitution**.

(2.10) $\sigma = \Delta(K/L) / (K/L) \div \Delta(MRTS_{L \text{ for } K}) / MRTS_{L \text{ for } K}$

Since in competitive equilibrium $MRTS_{L \text{ for } K} = MP_L / MP_K$ (see Chapter 4), the
elasticity of substitution is usually written:

(2.11) $\sigma = \% \Delta(K/L) \div \% \Delta[(MP_L / MP_K)]$

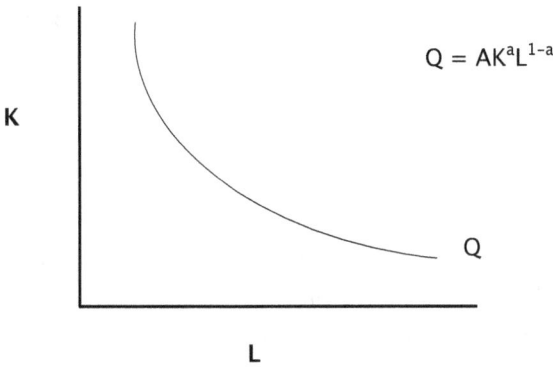

Figure 2.5. A Cobb–Douglass production function

The elasticity of substitution is the percent change in the ratio of the inputs used, divided by the percent change in the ratio of their marginal products. It shows how a change in the relative productivities of two inputs changes the relative amount used of those inputs.

When we bring prices into our basic model we will see that, assuming competitive equilibrium in the input market, the ratio of marginal products of the inputs will equal the ratio of their prices. So the elasticity of substitution shows how easy it is to substitute one input for another as their relative prices (in competitive equilibrium, this is equal to their relative marginal products) change. The three functional forms above have very different elasticities of substitution, reflecting the assumptions about production technology built into the production functions. A linear production function has an almost infinite elasticity of substitution because output can be easily increased by increasing either input without using more of the other. In fact it is possible to produce the good using only capital or only labor. The Leontief function has an elasticity of substitution of zero because an increase in both inputs in the same proportions is necessary to increase output. The Cobb–Douglas function has an elasticity of substitution equal to one, meaning that if the marginal product of labor increases by 10 percent relative to the marginal product of capital, then the amount of labor used increases by 10 percent relative to the amount of capital used.

It is worth going into a little more detail about the mathematics of the Cobb–Douglas function because it illustrates the power and convenience of the production function approach, and also the hidden dangers of building in assumptions about the nature of the production process based primarily on mathematical convenience. A typical way to write the Cobb–Douglas production function is:

(2.12) $Q = AK^a L^{1-a}, 0 < a < 1$

In this form, the Cobb–Douglas function exhibits **constant returns to scale**. If capital and labor are both increased by the same percentage, output also increases by the percentage. A 10 percent increase in both capital and labor means that output will increase by 10 percent. In mathematical jargon, this function is *linearly homogeneous*.

Another property of the Cobb–Douglas function is that the average products of capital and labor (Q/L) and (Q/K) and their marginal products (dQ/dL) and (dQ/dK) depend on the ratio in which capital and labor are used (K/L). To prove this, we can rewrite equation (2.7) as:

(2.13) $Q = AK^a L^{1-a} = A(K/L)^a L$

Then the average products of labor and capital are:

(2.14) $Q/L = A(K/L)^a (L/L) = A(K/L)^a$

(2.15) $Q/K = A(K/L)^a(L/K) = A(K/L)^a(K/L)^{-1} = A(K/L)^{a-1}$

And the marginal products become:

(2.16) $dQ/dL = (1-a) AK^a L^{1-a-1} = (1-a)A(K/L)^a$

(2.17) $dQ/dK = AK^{a-1} L^{1-a} = aA(K/L)^{a-1}$ (aA can be written as A, because both a and A represent some unknown constant)

Yet another property of the Cobb–Douglas function is that the elasticity of substitution is always equal to unity. Using equation (2.6), the elasticity of substitution can be written as:

(2.18) $\sigma = d(K/L)/(K/L) \div d(MP_L/MP_K)/(MP_L/MP_K)$

Let s be the MRTS between capital and labor, which, as we learned, is equal to the ratio of marginal products of K and L. Letting $k = K/L$ and using (2.11) and (2.12) gives us:

(2.19) $s=(1-a)A(K/L)^a/aA(K/L)^{a-1}=[(1-a)/a]k$

(2.20) $ds/dk=[(1-a)/a]$

Rewrite equation (2.13) as:

(2.21) $\sigma=dk/ds \div s/k$, or

(2.22) $\sigma=[a/1-a] \ [k/(1-a/a)k]=1$

This mathematical property implies that it is easy to substitute one input for another in production. A 10 percent increase in the marginal product of capital relative to the marginal product of labor will result in a 10 percent increase in the use of capital relative to the use of labor.

Another property of the Cobb–Douglas function is that the exponents of K and L represent each factor's share of total output if the factors are paid according to their marginal products. To show this we need to invoke **Euler's theorem,** which relates to a property of a **homogeneous function.** A function $Y=f(x1, x2, \ldots xn)$ is homogeneous of degree r, if it can be written as:

(2.23) $f(cx1, cx2, \ldots cxn)=c^r \ f(x1, x2, \ldots xn)$

Homogeneity means that if every term in the function is multiplied by some constant c, then the total value of the function will increase by the amount c^r, where r is the degree of homogeneity. For example, a production function exhibiting constant returns to scale is homogeneous of degree 1 ($r=1$). If all inputs are increased by, say, 10 percent, total output will increase by 10 percent. For such a constant returns to scale production function ($r=1$), $Q=f(K,L)$, Euler's theorem implies:

(2.24) $K(dQ/dK)+L(dQ/dL) \equiv Q$

The amount of capital used times the marginal product of capital plus the amount of labor used times the marginal product of labor will exactly equal total output. Expressed in physical units this means that if this were a production function for corn, and the factors of production were paid in corn, paying each factor according to its marginal product would exactly exhaust the output of corn during the time period of production. In Chapter 4, when we bring in money and prices, we will see that in a competitive economy in the long run, factors of production are paid according to their marginal products. According to the results of Euler's theorem, this means that total output will be exactly used up if it is distributed to the factors producing that output according to the condition: factor price=value of the marginal product. We will return to this idea in Chapter 4 when we discuss the characteristics of a competitive economy.

Finally, we can use the results above to show another property of the Cobb–Douglas function. The exponents a and $1-a$ are the output shares of capital and labor.

For capital we have:

$$(2.25) \quad K(dQ/dK)/Q = K\,aA(K/L)^{a-1}/Q = aKAk^{a-1}/LAk^a$$
$$= akAk^{a-1}/Ak^a = a$$

For labor the proof is:

$$(2.26) \quad L(dQ/dL)/Q = L(1-a)A(K/L)^a/Q = L(1-a)Ak^a/LAk^a = 1-a$$

The convenient mathematical properties of the Cobb–Douglas function have made it a real workhorse for use in statistical economic analysis. Variations of the Cobb–Douglas production function are still widely used, particularly in **total factor productivity** analysis (see the appendix).

The history of production function analysis can be seen as a steady relaxation of the restrictions of the Cobb–Douglas function. One step toward generality was relaxing the assumption that the coefficients must sum to one. A general form of the Cobb–Douglas function is:

$$(2.27) \quad Q = AK^aL^b$$

In the general form, $a+b$ is allowed to take on any value and indicates the degree of homogeneity of the function and the returns to scale of the production process it represents. If $a+b>1$ this indicates increasing returns to scale—double all inputs and output more than doubles. If $a+b<1$ this indicates decreasing returns to scale. Double all the inputs and output will increase by some factor less than that.

A production function that became popular in the 1960s is the CES, or constant elasticity of substitution function:

(2.28) $Q = \gamma[\delta K^{-\rho} + (1-\delta)L^{-\rho}]^{-1/\rho}$ where $\rho > -1$ and $\rho \neq 0$

In this equation, δ is a distribution parameter indicating the relative amounts of capital and labor, and ρ is a substitution parameter determining the value of the elasticity of substitution according to $\sigma = 1/(1+\rho)$. The CES function is more flexible than the Cobb–Douglas because the elasticity of substitution $(1/1-\rho)$ is not constrained to take on any particular value. However, whatever value it takes must be the same for any pair of inputs. For example, if we include three inputs, capital, labor, and energy, the elasticity of substitution between capital and labor, capital and energy, and energy and labor are all identical.

In the 1970s, a more flexible functional form of the production function came into fashion—the transcendental logarithmic function, or translog function. It is what is known as a Taylor's expansion of the general production function $Q = f(X1, X2, \ldots Xn)$. For the two input case we have been considering, it can be written as:

(2.29) $\log Q = \log\gamma_0 + \alpha_1\log K + \beta_1\log L + \alpha_2(\log K)^2 +$
            $\beta_2(\log L)^2 + \gamma_1\log K\log L$

The difficulty with the translog function is that it is very sensitive to the data used to estimate it. In time series estimates, small changes in the amounts of capital and labor can produce wide variations in the elasticity of substitution between inputs.

▶ **ASSUMPTION ALERT!** *Things to think about before moving on.*

The neoclassical theory of production is a model of the static exchange of a fixed amount of inputs among firms with given techniques of production and each firm having (implicitly) perfect information about the characteristics of the inputs and the production techniques available.

The particular Pareto-efficient outcome depends on the initial distribution of the inputs among the two firms. ◀

So far we have said nothing about prices, wages, or economic rent. No money has been involved, just physical relationships among inputs. Surprisingly, we will see that although microeconomic theory is sometimes called "price theory," in the pure Walrasian model money plays no independent role. As we will see later, this has surprising implications for neoclassical macroeconomics.

APPENDIX

Separability

It is frequently useful when analyzing a particular production process to separate that process into stages or components. For example, making a bicycle might involve making the chassis, wheels, seat, and pedals and putting them all together at the end (Figure 2.6).

In the production function framework, a technology is said to be separable if the marginal rate of technical substitution between two inputs in one technology (making the bicycle wheels, for example) is unaffected by changes in the levels of other inputs.

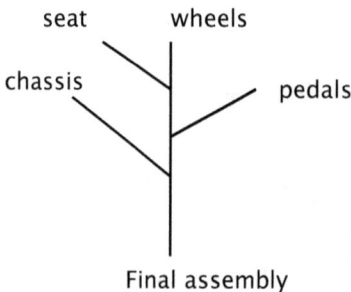

Figure 2.6. Separating assembly of a bicycle into discrete technologies

The Solow Growth Model and Total Factor Productivity

In 1957 Robert Solow developed a "dynamic" version of the Cobb–Douglas function. Solow's model essentially allocates the *growth rates* of inputs and outputs instead of the absolute amounts of inputs. Solow used the neoclassical production function to explore the relationship between the growth of output per worker (Q/L) and the growth of the capital labor ratio (K/L). Solow's work helped earn him a Nobel Prize in economics and laid the groundwork for the **microfoundations project** in economics, that is, establishing the rules of behavior for the macroeconomy based on the microeconomic theory of the firm.

Stated in terms of rates of growth, the Cobb–Douglas function becomes:

(2.30) $\quad \dot{Q} = A \dot{K}^a \dot{L}^{1-a}$.

A dot ($\bullet$) over K, L, or Q indicates that variable's rate of growth (Figure 2.7). Equation (2.31) can be used to illustrate the concept of *total factor productivity* (TFP).

Total factor productivity (TFP) is written as:

(2.31) $\quad \dot{A} = \dot{Q} - a\dot{K} - (1-a)\dot{L}$

The weights a and $(1-a)$ are the product shares of capital and labor. As we will see later, in competitive equilibrium these are equal to the cost shares of K and L. Notice three things about the TFP measure:

1. It is calculated as a *residual*, that is, the portion of the growth rate in output not accounted for by the weighted growth rates of the inputs of capital and labor.

2. The relative importance of the inputs of capital and labor is indicated by their output shares. These are calculated based on the assumption of linear homogeneity (constant returns to scale).

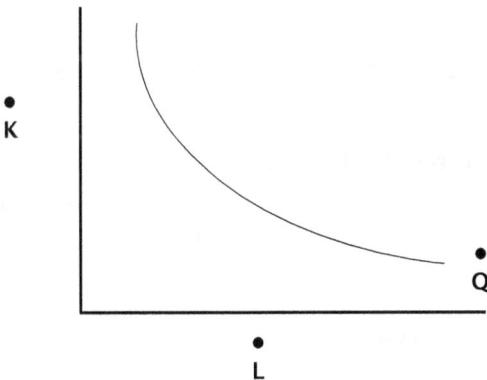

Figure 2.7. A production function in terms of growth rates

3. TFP is a reformulation of the static model of optimal allocation, using input growth rates rather than the absolute amounts of the inputs.

GLOSSARY

Constant returns to scale—If all inputs are increased by the same percentage, output will increase by that percentage. This is the mathematical property of being linearly homogeneous or homogenous of degree 1.

Contract curve for production—The locus of all Pareto-efficient points in an Edgeworth box diagram, each point representing a different initial distribution of inputs. At each point on the contract curve, the marginal rates of technical substitution between the two inputs are the same for the two producers.

Diminishing marginal productivity—As more and more of one input is used, the amounts of all other inputs held constant, the point will be reached where the increase in output from an additional unit of that input begins to decline.

Diminishing marginal rate of technical substitution—As the amount of one input increases relative to another input, the more of the first input a producer is willing to give up in exchange for the second input.

Elasticity of substitution—A mathematical expression indicating the ability of a firm (with a given technology) to substitute one input for another in production.

Euler's theorem—If a function such as $Q = f(K,L)$ is homogeneous of degree r, then we can write: $K(dQ/dK) + L(dQ/dL) \equiv rQ$

Homogeneous function—A function $Y = f(x1, x2, \ldots xn)$ is homogeneous of degree r if it can be written as: $f(cx1, cx2, \ldots cxn) = c^r f(x1, x2, \ldots xn)$. Homogeneity means that if every term in the function is multiplied by some constant c, then the total value of the function will increase by the amount c^r.

Isoquant—A curve showing all the combinations of two inputs yielding the same level of output.

Marginal product—The additional output obtained from one additional unit of a productive input, the amounts of all other inputs held constant.

Marginal rate of technical substitution—The rate at which one input can be substituted for another keeping total output constant.

Microfoundations project—The use of the Walrasian theory of the firm to describe the macroeconomy.

Pareto efficiency in exchange—In production, a situation in which no further trading of inputs can increase the output of one good without decreasing the output of another good.

Production function—Expresses output as a function of the quantities of inputs used. In this chapter, we have seen the general form $Q = f(K, L)$. Three popular forms are the Cobb–Douglas, CES, and translog functions.

Total factor productivity—The growth rate in output not accounted for by the growth rates of inputs. It is taken to be a measure of technological change.

GENERAL EQUILIBRIUM
IN A BARTER ECONOMY

Exchange is political economy, it is society itself, for it is impossible
to conceive of society without exchange or exchange without society.
—*Frédéric Bastiat*, Economic Harmonies *[1850], translated from the French
by W. Hayden Boyers, edited by George B. de Huszar (Princeton, NJ: Van
Nostrand, 1964), xxv*

The major concern of Walrasian economic theory is efficiency. In Chapter 1 we established the condition for Pareto efficiency with respect to consumers exchanging market goods, namely, that the marginal rates of substitution (MRS) for the goods should be the same for both consumers. In Chapter 2 we established the condition for Pareto efficiency in production, namely, that the marginal rates of technical substitution (MRTS) for the inputs used in production should be the same for the two firms. The third and final step in our discussion of a barter economy is to establish the conditions for efficiency in general. How can we know that firms are efficiently producing the array of goods that consumers value most highly? In economic jargon, how do we know the economy is in **general equilibrium?** When an economy is in general equilibrium, the array of goods that consumers *want* (given their preferences) is the same as the array that producers *can* produce (with given technologies).

To establish general equilibrium between producers and consumers (general or *global* Pareto efficiency) we need three analytical tools: a **utility possibilities frontier**, a **production possibilities frontier**, and a **social welfare function**.

THE UTILITY POSSIBILITIES FRONTIER

As we saw in Chapter 1, employing the criterion of Pareto efficiency in exchange requires starting with a particular distribution of the two goods between the

two consumers. Referring to the *consumption space* diagram in Figure 3.1, a different initial distribution of the goods will result in a different Pareto-efficient point along the contract curve CC'. All the points on the contract curve are Pareto efficient, so how do we determine which distribution of the two goods maximizes social welfare in our simple two-person society? To answer this question, we begin by converting the commodity consumption of our two consumers into a measure of their relative utilities. Notice in the consumption space diagram in Figure 3.1 that at point 3 consumer A has more of both goods X and Y and at point 1 consumer B has more of both goods. At point 2 the goods are evenly distributed. Assuming that commodity consumption is equivalent to utility, we can use this information to construct a second diagram showing the relative utilities of A and B at each point on the contract curve. This is called a **utility possibilities frontier**. It shows the relative utilities of A and B for every possible Pareto-efficient distribution of the two goods.

THE PRODUCTION POSSIBILITIES FRONTIER

The next thing we need is a **production possibilities frontier**. This can be derived from the Edgeworth box for production showing the exchange of inputs between firms. Along the contract curve showing all the different

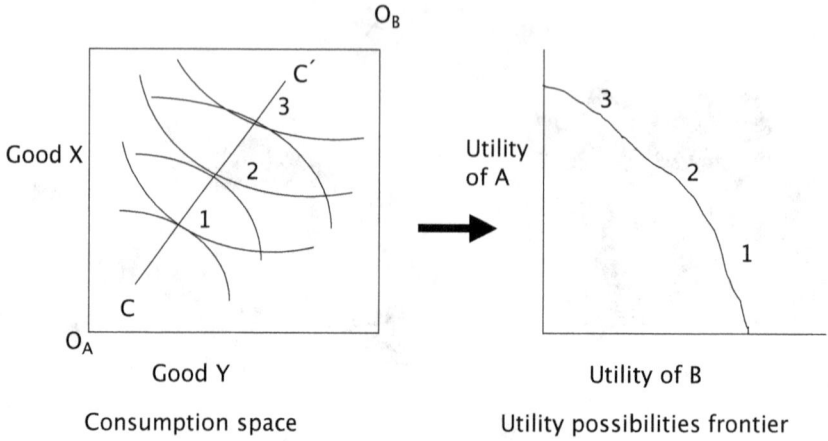

Figure 3.1. From commodity consumption to utility possibilities

Pareto-efficient combinations of K and L, notice that at point 3 in the *input space* box in Figure 3.2, most of the capital and labor available in this simple economy is used to produce good X. At point 1 most of the two inputs are used to produce good Y. This information can be transferred to the diagram on the right in Figure 3.2 showing the production possibilities frontier (PPF). The PPF shows the maximum amount of one good that can be produced given the amount produced of the other good.

Any point on the production possibilities frontier can be used to generate an Edgeworth box for consumption as shown for two points in the diagram on the left in Figure 3.3. The two Edgeworth boxes on the left in Figure 3.3 are the same as the ones in Chapter 1 (figures 1.2 and 1.3). Remember that one of the starting points for this analysis is that the total amounts of goods X and Y are fixed. All the possible combinations of X and Y are given by the points on the production possibilities frontier, and each one of these will generate a different Edgeworth box in consumption space and a different contract curve. These contract curves can be transformed into utility possibility curves as shown in Figure 3.3. Using all these utility possibility curves we can take one more step—applying the Pareto principle one more time—and construct a **grand utility possibilities frontier** (GUPF). The GUPF is an envelope

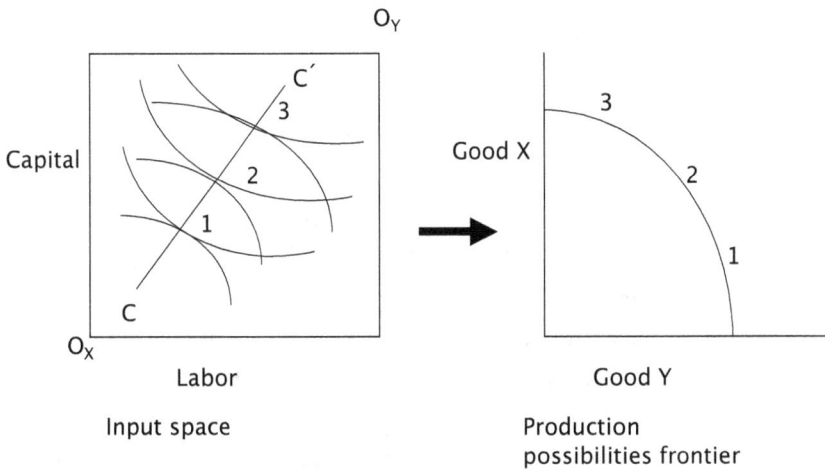

Figure 3.2. From input allocation to production

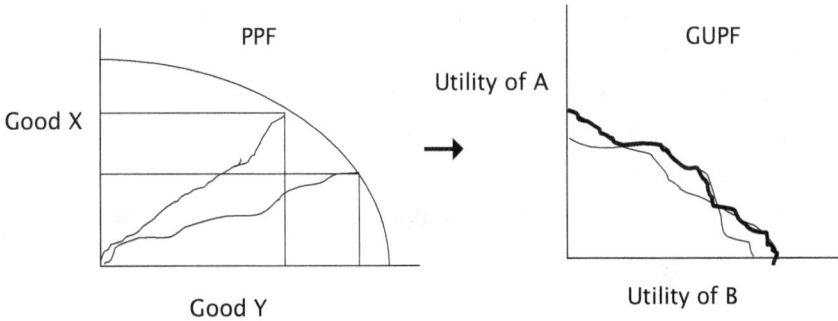

Figure 3.3. From the production possibilities frontier to the grand utility possibilities frontier

curve derived from the various utility possibility curves such as the two shown in the right-hand diagram in Figure 3.3. If we are on a curve below the GUPF (the heavy shaded line in the right-hand diagram in Figure 3.3), we can increase the utility of either A or B (or both) without decreasing the utility of either one.

THE SOCIAL WELFARE FUNCTION

Once we have constructed the grand utility possibility frontier, we have reached the limit to applying the Pareto principle. All points on the GUPF are Pareto optimal and we have no method or rule to pick one point over another. Any movement along the GUPF will make one of the consumers, either A or B, worse off. To pick the "best" point on the GUPF, that is, to choose the "socially optimal" combination of the utilities of consumers A and B, we need a **social welfare function** such as the one depicted in Figure 3.4.

Social welfare functions such as those labeled SWF1, SWF2, and SWF3 show all the combinations of utilities of A and B that are equally acceptable from society's point of view. As is the case with individual utility functions, social welfare functions further away from the origin represent higher levels of utility. In Figure 3.4, society's utility is maximized a point 1 where the social welfare function SWF2 is tangent to the grand utility possibilities frontier. This is called a *constrained bliss point*. Moving from point 2 on social welfare function SWF1 to point 1 on the higher social welfare function SWF2 increases society's total well-being. Point 3 on social welfare function SWF3 is unattainable given society's limited technology and resources.

The unspecified neoclassical (or "Bergsonian," after economist Abram Bergson) social welfare function is the weighted sum of individual welfares:

(3.1) $W = \Sigma \, k(i)U(i)$

The weights k(i) are unspecified, but neoclassical economists point out that any specification of the function will make neoclassical welfare theory a complete theory of social choice.

There are many possibilities and difficulties in constructing a social welfare function. The basic question is, how should society "choose" among the many possible Pareto-efficient distributions of income? We look at two possibilities here just for purposes of illustration. One possibility is just to accept the existing distribution of income, whatever it is, as "fair." This is essentially the position of Robert Nozick's *contractarian* approach (see his book *Anarchy, State, and Utopia*, 1974), which argues society has a set of rules for acquiring wealth. People who are wealthy have gained their wealth by following

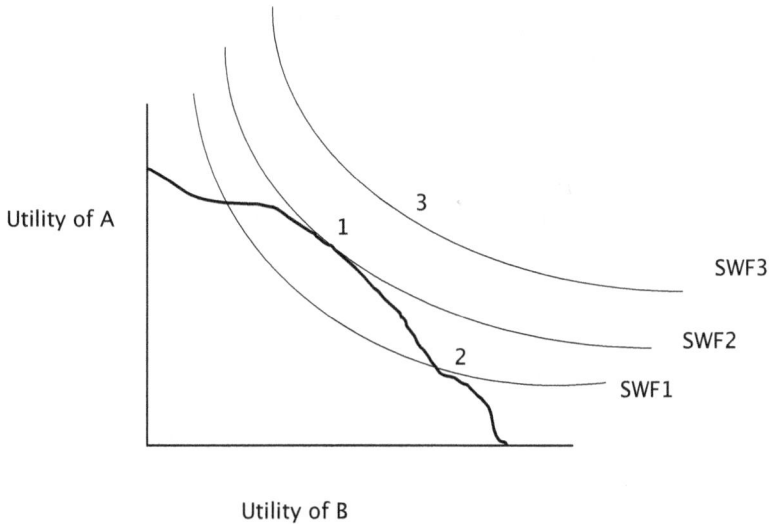

Figure 3.4. Social welfare functions

these rules, and taking money away from them and giving it to those who have not followed the rules (the poor, for example) represents an unfair taking of property—a breach of the social contract.

John Rawls, in his book *A Theory of Justice* (1971), takes a much different approach. He conducts a thought experiment and asks the question, if you had a choice of being placed in one of many different societies, each with a different income distribution, from very equal to very unequal, and you did not know ahead of time what your income would be, what sort of income distribution would you choose? Consider, for example, the points on the contract curve in Figure 3.1. If you did not know ahead of time whether your position in this society would be consumer A or consumer B, which point would you choose? Point 1 where consumer B has most of the two goods, point 3 where consumer A has most of the two goods, or point 2 where the goods are about evenly distributed? Both from a sense of fairness and a tendency toward loss aversion, most people would pick point 2.

There exists a vast literature on social welfare functions (and on the work Nozick and Rawls), and these simple examples are only an introduction to the complexity of the issue of social justice. But before we leave the issue, we need to mention the **Arrow impossibility theorem**. Basically, Arrow's theorem shows that there is no way to convert the rankings of individual preferences into a social (community-wide) ranking, given a few basic and reasonable assumptions. These include non-dictatorship, universality, and independence of irrelevant alternatives. Once again, a vast literature examines and extends Arrow's theorem. The problem raised by Arrow's theorem, like so many other difficulties in the Walrasian system, arises from the assumption of atomistic agents, that is, the "voters" (or coalitions of voters) must act independently of other voters. Arrow's paradox is discussed in more detail in Chapter 6.

THE THIRD CONDITION FOR PARETO EFFICIENCY IN EXCHANGE

To establish the final condition for Pareto efficiency in a pure exchange economy, we need to start with a point on the production possibilities frontier (Figure 3.2). This point indicates the total amounts of goods X and Y that our simple economy can produce given its technology and available resources. Each point corresponds to an Edgeworth box diagram showing all the Pareto-efficient distributions of those goods X and Y between the two consumers (the contract curve).

The slope of the production possibilities frontier gives the *rate of product transformation* (RPT), that is, the rate at which the output of one good can be reduced thereby freeing up resources that can be used to increase the output of the other good. For example if the slope of the PPF is 1, this indicates that we can give up one unit of good X and produce one more unit of good Y. It shows the rate at which our economy is *able* to switch production for one good to the other, given the available resources and technology. Now consider the points on the contract curve for exchange (in the Edgeworth box within the PPF) in Figure 3.5. All these points correspond to points of tangency of the indifference cures for the two consumers, that is, points where the marginal rates of substitution (MRS) for the two goods are the same for both consumers. In other words, these points show the rate at which our simple society is *willing* to substitute one good for another, given the preferences

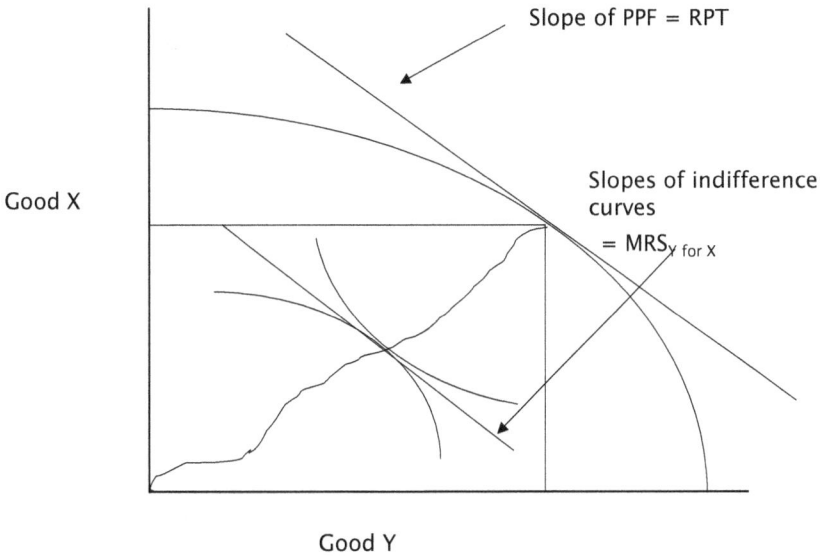

Figure 3.5. General equilibrium in a pure exchange economy

of our two consumers. This leads to the third Pareto condition for efficiency. The rate at which society is able to substitute one good for another in production must be equal to the rate at which consumers are willing to substitute one good for another in consumption.

(3.2) $MRS_{Y \text{ for } X} = RPT_{Y \text{ for } X}$

The best way to convince yourself that this is true is to consider a situation in which this is not the case. Assume that the $RPT_{Y \text{ for } X}$ is equal to two; for example, our society can produce two more apples by giving up the production of one orange. Assume further that the marginal rate of substitution is equal to one. That is, consumers are willing to give up one orange for one apple. If this is the case, then our economy can give up the production of one orange, use the freed up resources to produce two apples, and thereby make consumers happier. They are "better off" by one apple. As long as the $RPT \neq MRS$ there are efficiency gains to be obtained by changing the mix of the production of goods X and Y.

Pareto Condition III. *The third and final condition for Pareto efficiency in a barter economy is that the rate at which the economy can stop producing one good in order to produce more of the other good, the rate of product transformation (RPT), is equal to the rate at which consumers are willing to give up consumption of one good in order to consume more of the other good, the marginal rate of substitution (MRS). When this condition is fulfilled the economy is in a state of general equilibrium.*

Given all the assumptions about the nature of preferences, the substitutability of inputs, the complete assignment of property rights, the unrestricted availability of information, and so on, we end up with the following situation.

1. Consumers are maximizing their well-being by getting the most desirable array of goods possible, given their stable preferences and their initial endowments of these goods.

2. Producers are maximizing the output of the goods they produce, given the state of technology and their initial endowment of productive inputs.

3. For any particular output of X and Y, this system will ensure not only that these goods are produced in the most efficient manner possible but also that the distribution of the goods between the consumers is the most efficient possible.

To summarize the conditions for Pareto efficiency we have established:

Pareto Condition I: In consumption, the marginal rates of substitution between the two goods are the same for the two consumers.

$$\overset{\text{A}}{\text{MRS}}_{\text{Y for X}} = \overset{\text{B}}{\text{MRS}}_{\text{Y for X}}$$

Pareto Condition II: In production, the marginal rates of technical substitution between the two inputs goods are the same for both producers.

$$\overset{\text{X}}{\text{MRTS}}_{\text{L for K}} = \overset{\text{Y}}{\text{MRTS}}_{\text{L for K}}$$

Pareto Condition III: General Pareto efficiency occurs when the rate at which consumers are willing to substitute one good for another in consumption is the same as the rate at which producers can switch from making one good to making another in production.

A=B

$$MRS_{X \text{ for } Y} = RPT_{Y \text{ for } X}$$

▶ **ASSUMPTION ALERT!** *The conditions for establishing general equilibrium:*

1. *The economy is operating on the contract curve for the exchange of goods. No person's utility can be increased without reducing the utility of at least one other person. All the assumptions of Homo economicus hold.*

2. *The economy is operating on the contract curve for the exchange of inputs. The production of one good cannot be increased without decreasing the output of at least one other good. All the assumptions of perfect competition hold.*

3. *The economy is operating on the production possibilities frontier. Resources and technology are being employed in the most efficient way possible.* ◀

A POTENTIAL PARETO IMPROVEMENT

Before we move from our simple face-to-face barter economy to one that is based on price signals, we need one more concept. This is the notion of a **potential Pareto improvement,** or PPI, first proposed independently by John Hicks and Nicholas Kaldor in 1939. It is sometimes called the Kaldor–Hicks criterion or the compensation principle. A severe limitation of the strict Pareto criterion is its restricted policy applicability. Almost any action affecting the economy will benefit some people and harm others.

Suppose we are in a situation such as point 1 in Figure 3.6. This is a Pareto inferior situation, because we can move to any point in the hatched area and make both consumers better off. The thick line on the contract curve within the hatched area is called the **core** of an exchange economy. We can also say that a movement to any point in the dotted areas will make both consumers worse off. But what about a movement to a point such as point 2? This is a movement from a Pareto inferior to a Pareto-efficient point, but a movement from point 1 to point 2 will make consumer A worse off and is not permitted under the strict Pareto criterion.

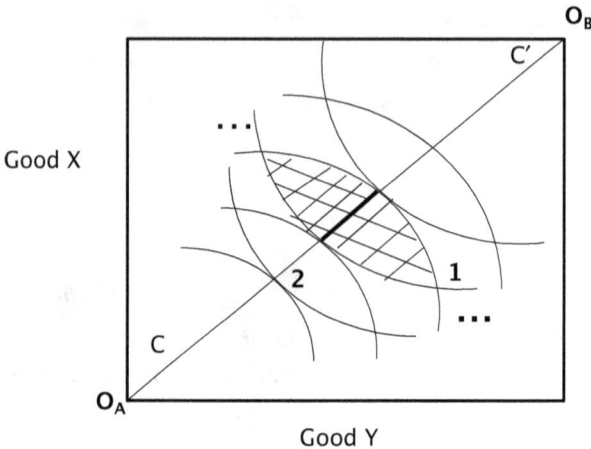

Figure 3.6. A potential Pareto improvement

The Kaldor–Hicks criterion permits such a move if the total change in utility is positive. Kaldor's version is that such a change should be made if the winner can compensate the loser and still be better off. Hicks's version is that a change should be made if the loser cannot bribe the winner not to make the change (and still be better off). According to Kaldor, whether or not the loser is actually compensated is irrelevant. Economists should be concerned with efficiency, not distribution. It is up to politicians to decide whether or not an outcome is fair.

The notion of a potential Pareto improvement revolutionized economics in two important ways. First of all, it legitimized the focus of economic analysis and economic policy on efficiency. Second, it paved the way for economists to focus on increasing per capita income as the major goal of economic policy. Identification of potential Pareto improvements, that is, efficiency gains, is the major task of cost-benefit analysis, one of the principal tools of economic analysis.

This completes our discussion of general equilibrium (Pareto efficiency or Pareto optimality) in a pure barter economy. Again, this model is the heart and soul of contemporary Walrasian economics. As the next chapter shows, the model of perfect competition adds prices and markets to the barter system but ends up with exactly the same conditions for economic efficiency. This model of a pure exchange economy is the ideal to which most economists consciously or unconsciously refer when making policy recommendations about actual economies.

APPENDIX

The Existence of Equilibrium

The intellectual power of the Walrasian system lies in the fact that, given all the assumptions about consumer and producer behavior and technology, we can find a unique efficient level and mix of output. That is, we can find a point where a given set of preferences and a given set of production possibilities meet.

As economics became more and more mathematical in the middle of the twentieth century, more attention was given to the mathematical properties of the equations describing market economies. A lot of attention was given to proving that, given the mathematical assumptions of the Walrasian system, it is mathematically possible to establish an equilibrium point where the set of commodities produced exactly duplicated the set of commodities

that consumers wanted. In particular, a branch of mathematics called topology can establish the conditions under which the set of consumer preferences and the set of producer possibilities meet at a unique point as shown in the diagram above. These are called **fixed-point theorems.** One basic proof is Brouwer's fixed-point theorem, which, stated formally, demonstrates that a continuous mapping of a closed, bounded convex set onto itself has a least one fixed point. Formally, there exists a point such that $f(x)=x$. Brouwer's proof was used to show that under the assumptions of the model of perfect competition, where utility and production functions are smooth and continuous, at least one equilibrium point exists where the set of production possibilities are the same as the set of consumption possibilities.

In Figure 3.7 the diagonal represents all the points where $x=x$, and the dotted line represents some mapping (transformation) of x, denoted by $f(x)$. In the diagram there is no way to draw a continuous line from the left vertical axis to the right vertical axis of the diagram without crossing the diagonal. When the dotted line crosses the diagonal, $f(x)=x$, and this proves that in the mathematical representation of the economy, there is at least one point where a general equilibrium solution exists. One problem with Brouwer's theorem is that other systems exist that do not satisfy the conditions of perfect competition but that also have equilibrium points. More general

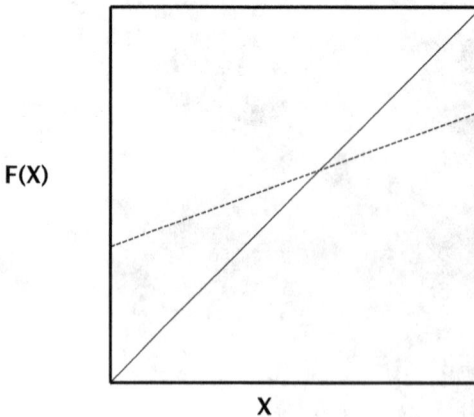

Figure 3.7. Brouwer's fixed-point theorem

versions of Brouwer's theorem are the Kakutani, Schauder, and Lefschetz fixed-point theorems.

GLOSSARY

Arrow impossibility theorem—Given the requirements of non-imposition, non-dictatorship, Pareto efficiency, and independence of irrelevant alternatives, no voting system can convert individual preferences into a society-wide ranking.

Core—In the Edgeworth box diagram, the core is the segment of the contract curve that contains all the reachable Pareto-efficient outcomes given the initial endowment.

Fixed-point theorems—Mathematical theorems used by economists to ensure the theoretical existence of a point of general equilibrium.

General equilibrium—A situation in which consumers are maximizing their utility given their initial endowment of goods, producers are maximizing output given their initial endowment of productive inputs, and producers are producing the most desirable mix of goods based on consumer preferences.

Grand utility possibilities frontier—A graph or curve showing the maximum possible utility of one person given the utility of the other person. It is an envelop curve derived from all the utility possibilities frontier curves associated with every possible contract curve for consumption.

Potential Pareto improvement—A gain in total utility that makes at least one person worse off. Sometimes it is called the compensation principle or the Kaldor–Hicks criterion.

Production possibilities frontier—A graph or curve showing the maximum possible production of one good given the production of the other good. It shows all the Pareto-efficient combinations of goods that can be produced, given society's endowment of resources and technology.

Rate of product transformation—The rate at which an economy can switch from producing one to good to another. It is equal to the slope of the production possibilities frontier.

Social welfare function—A graph or curve showing the all the possible combinations of individual utilities where social welfare is the same. The social welfare function is based on given preferences, technology and resource endowment, plus some specific ethical assumption about the fair distribution of goods among consumers.

Utility possibilities frontier—A graph or curve showing the maximum possible utility of one consumer given the utility of the other consumer. It shows all the possible Pareto-efficient combinations of utilities, given the preferences of each consumer.

REFERENCES

Nozick, Robert. 1974. *Anarchy, State and Utopia*. New York: Basic Books.
Rawls, John. 1971. *A Theory of Justice*. Cambridge, MA: Harvard University
     Press.

4

INTRODUCING PRICES

Perfect Competition and

Pareto Efficiency

As every individual, therefore, endeavours as much as he can both
to employ his capital in the support of domestick industry, and so
to direct that industry that its produce may be of the greatest value;
every individual necessarily labours to render the annual revenue of
the society as great as he can. He generally, indeed, neither intends
to promote the publick interest, nor knows how much he is
promoting it. By preferring the support of domestick to that of
foreign industry, he intends only his own security; and by directing
that industry in such a manner as its produce may be of the greatest
value, he intends only his own gain, and he is in this, as in many
other cases, led by an invisible hand to promote an end which was
no part of his intention.
> —*Adam Smith,* An Inquiry into the Nature and Causes of the Wealth of
> Nations *[1776], edited by R. H. Campbell and A. S. Skinner (New York:*
> *Liberty Press, 1981, IV.ii), 456*

The Walrasian representation of a barter economy presented in chapters 1–3
is the core of contemporary microeconomic theory. Interestingly, although
microeconomics is sometimes called "price theory," prices play no independent role in the basic Walrasian system. In a "frictionless" economy popu-
lated by independent consumers and producers with perfect information
about prices, the results of free exchange will exactly duplicate the outcome
obtained in a face-to-face barter system. The price of each good contains all
the information necessary to compare its desirability to the desirability of
every other good. In such an economy the "invisible hand" of the market will
ensure the most efficient allocation of society's scarce resources.

STEP ONE: MAXIMIZING UTILITY SUBJECT
TO A BUDGET CONSTRAINT

Let us begin by adding prices to the consumer choice model in Chapter 1. Let us give the consumer a budget (call it M for "money") to spend and an array of goods (with prices) to choose from. How does a consumer allocate his or her income among various consumer goods so as to maximize the utility the consumer receives from these goods?

Given a budget M and the prices of goods X (P_x) and Y (P_Y), how does a consumer decide how much of each good to buy? As shown in Figure 4.1, this consumer's utility is maximized at point 1 where the indifference curve I2 is just tangent to the budget line showing all the possible combinations of the goods X and Y the consumer could buy given the consumer's income the relative prices of the goods. At point 1, the consumer buys ten units of each good. Given the budget line, the consumer could have chosen point 2 but can increase his or her utility by moving to point 1 instead (on the higher indifference curve I2). Any point on the higher indifference curve I3 would be preferred to point 1, but those choices are unavailable given the budget constraint.

Chapter 1 showed that the slope of the indifference curve is equal to the marginal rate of substitution ($MRS_{Y \text{ for } X}$), which is equal to the ratio of the

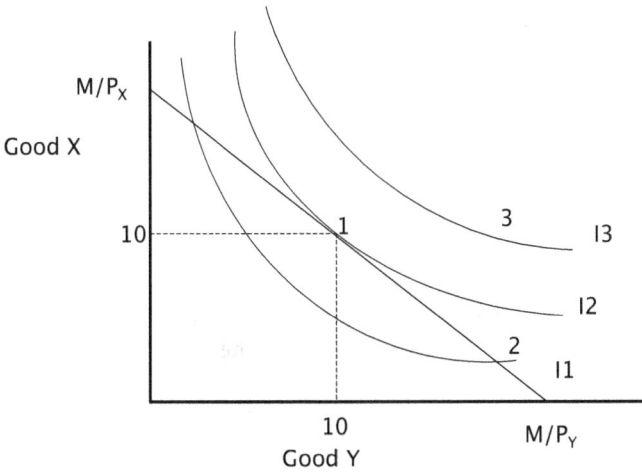

Figure 4.1. Maximizing utility subject to a budget constraint

marginal utilities of the two goods. The equation for the budget constraint is $M = P_X X + P_Y Y$. Rearranging terms to express the budget in terms of goods X and Y yields:

(4.1) $X = M/P_X - (P_Y/P_X)Y$

The intercept M/P_X shows how many units of good X could be purchased if the consumer spent his or her entire budget on good X. Equation (4.1) shows that the slope of the budget line is equal to the price ratio of the two goods:

(4.2) $dX/dY = -P_Y/P_X$

So the condition for utility maximization, that the indifference curve is just tangent to the budget line, is:

(4.3) $P_Y/P_X = MRS_{Y \text{ for } X} = MU_Y/MU_X$

We can obtain this result using the mathematics of constrained optimization. The Lagrangian equation (see the appendix at the end of this chapter) for maximizing utility subject to a budget constraint is:

(4.4) $Z = U(X, Y) - \lambda(P_X X + P_Y Y - M)$

Taking the partial derivatives of this equation and setting them to zero yields:

(4.5) $\partial Z / \partial X = \partial U / \partial X - \lambda P_X = 0$

(4.6) $\partial Z / \partial Y = \partial U / \partial Y - \lambda P_Y = 0$

(4.7) $\partial Z / \partial \lambda = M - P_X X - P_Y Y = 0$

Moving the second term in the first two equations to the right-hand side and dividing the first equation by the second gives us the **first-order condition** for maximizing utility subject to a budget constraint:

(4.8) $(\partial U / \partial X) / (\partial U / \partial Y) = P_X / P_Y$

As demonstrated in Figure 4.1, the ratio of marginal utilities of the two goods must equal their price ratio. To ensure that this condition maximizes utility (rather than minimizing it) we need the **second-order condition**:

(4.9) $d^2 U / dX^2 = \partial^2 U / \partial X^2 + 2 \, (\partial^2 U / \partial X \partial \delta Y)(-P_X / P_Y)$
$$+ (\partial^2 U / \partial Y^2) \, P_X^2 < 0$$

It can also be shown that in equilibrium $\lambda = (\partial U / \partial X) / P_X = (\partial U / \partial Y) / P_Y$, that is, the Lagrangian multiplier equals the marginal utility of each good divided by its price. This means that, when the consumer is maximizing utility subject to a budget constraint, the consumer gets the same utility from a dollar spent on each good. So λ can be interpreted as the **marginal utility of money.**

STEP TWO: INPUTS, OUTPUT, AND MARGINAL COST

Let us now turn to the production side and reexamine the **production possibilities frontier** by adding the costs of production to our model. We saw in Chapter 3 that the slope of the production possibilities frontier indicates the **rate of product transformation**, that is, the rate at which the resources used in the production of one good can be shifted to the production of another good while maintaining the greatest output efficiency possible. In our simple model if we produce one fewer unit of good X, then this frees up capi-

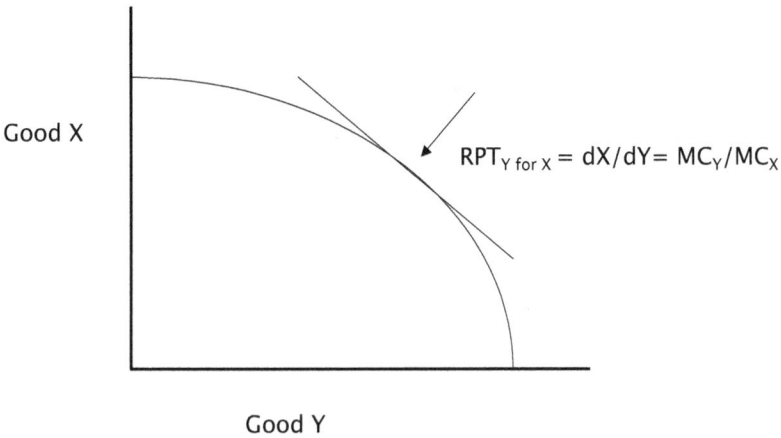

Figure 4.2. Marginal costs and the production possibilities frontier

tal and labor that can be used to produce good Y. For simplicity, assume that labor is the only productive input. Suppose that producing one more unit of good Y requires two units of labor and that producing one more unit of good X requires one unit of labor. So the marginal cost of producing Y is two and the marginal cost of X is one. As depicted in Figure 4.2, the ratio of marginal costs MC_Y / MC_X (two in this example) is also the rate of product transformation of X into Y. If we give up one unit of Y this frees up enough resources (two units of labor in our simple example) to produce two units of X.

$$(4.10) \quad RPT_{Y \text{ for } X} = MC_Y / MC_X$$

STEP THREE: PERFECT COMPETITION

The last piece of economic theory we need is the centerpiece of neoclassical microeconomics, the model of "pure" or "perfect" competition. The model of perfect competition is based on the following assumptions:

▶ **ASSUMPTION ALERT!** *Assumptions of the model of perfect competition:*

  1. *There exist very large numbers of buyers and sellers. No single buyer or seller can influence the price of any good or the actions of other buyers and sellers.*

2. *There exists perfect information, available to all, about the characteristics of all goods and productive inputs. The price of a good contains all the information necessary to judge its utility to any consumer.*

3. *There are no barriers to firms entering any market. Productive inputs are perfectly mobile so that they can migrate to their most productive use.*

4. *All firms within a particular industry are exactly identical. Within a particular industry, there is no reason for consumers to buy one good rather than another except on the basis of price.* ◄

Two critical assumptions of the model of perfect competition are rarely emphasized in economic textbooks: (1) prices carry all the information needed to assign goods and inputs to their most efficient uses and (2) there is no interaction among firms, that is, there is no real competition. Under the assumptions of perfect competition, the prices and quantities produced of each good are set by the forces of supply and demand in a particular industry (widgets, basketballs, or whatever) and those prices are taken by all firms in that industry. As depicted in Figure 4.3, the supply curve for the industry is upward sloping. This is because a higher price encourages more firms to enter the industry and thus increases the total output of the industry. The is sometimes called the **law of supply**, that is, price and quantity supplied or directly related, or $dQ_s / dP > 0$. The demand curve is downward sloping for two reasons: (1) as the price of good increases, consumers switch to other products

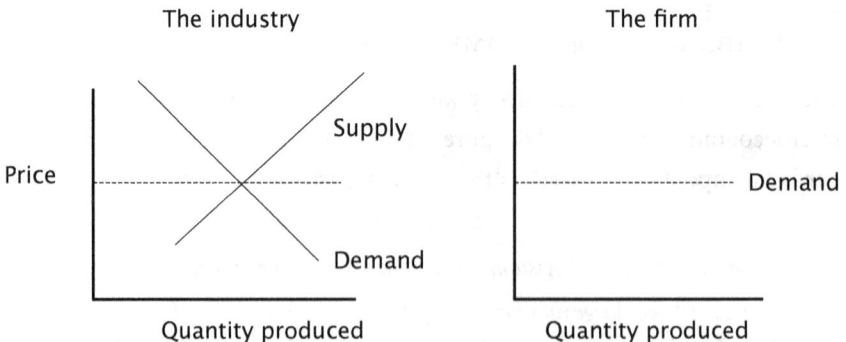

Figure 4.3. Industries and firms in a competitive market

and (2) as prices increase, a consumer's real income decreases and the consumer purchases less of the good (if the good is a "normal" good, see the discussion of the income and substitution effects in the next chapter). The **law of demand** states that the price and the quantity supplied of a good are inversely related, or $dQ_d / dP < 0$.

In a perfectly competitive market, the firm is a price taker, that is, the price of the good is outside the control of the firm. There is no incentive for a firm to change its price. If it were to raise its price, given the assumptions of the model, its sales would fall to zero because consumers could buy an identical good from another firm at a lower price. There is no reason for a firm to lower its price because it can sell all it produces at the prevailing market price. In economic jargon, the demand curve for a competitive firm is perfectly elastic.

The properties of this model are discussed in countless textbooks and they will not be repeated in detail here. To continue our discussion of Pareto optimality and competition, the main result of this model is that in long-run competitive equilibrium the marginal cost of producing a good is exactly equal to the marginal revenue gained from selling it. This occurs at point e in Figure 4.4. Anywhere to the right of point e, the costs of producing one more unit of the good are higher than the revenue obtained from selling it. Anywhere to the left of point e, the cost of producing one more unit is less than the revenue obtained from selling. So if the firm is producing any output not exactly equal to the equilibrium quantity Q^e, then there is an incentive for the firm to change its output and move to that point.

Firms in long-run competitive equilibrium do not make an **economic profit,** defined as any profit over and above the average rate of profit prevailing in the economy. All firms make the same **accounting profit,** which does not include the **opportunity cost** of producing in the next most profitable industry. For example, if a firm makes an accounting profit of 10 percent and the average rate of profit is 9 percent, then that firm is making an economic profit of 1 percent (accounting profit minus opportunity cost). A firm earning 8 percent would have an economic loss of 1 percent. It could be making more money by moving to another industry.

Another important property of the competitive model is that the firm is producing at the minimum point on the long-run average cost (LRAC) curve.

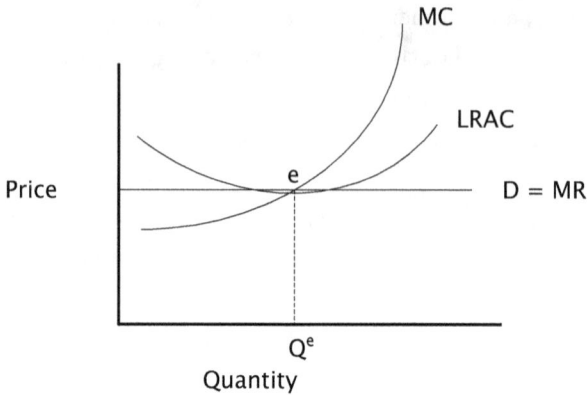

Figure 4.4. Long-run competitive equilibrium

That is, the firm is producing the product at the lowest possible cost, given society's resources and technology. Given the assumptions of the model, every firm in a particular market must be using the most efficient production technique possible or it will be driven out of business by other more efficient firms that can produce the same good at a lower cost and sell it for a lower price. At the minimum point on the long-run average cost curve, that curve is just tangent to the (horizontal) demand curve. If the LRAC curve were above the demand curve, the firm would be operating at a loss because the unit cost of producing the good would be higher than the price received for the good. Firms would leave the industry and the price of the good would rise until the LRAC was just tangent to the demand curve. If the LRAC curve were below the demand curve, the firm would be operating at a profit because the unit cost of producing the good would be lower than the price received for the good. In this case firms would enter the industry, thereby lowering the market price of the good until the demand curve for the firm becomes just tangent to the LRAC curve.

So under the assumptions of perfect competition, market forces ensure that (1) the firm is operating as efficiently as possible, and (2) the price of the good is exactly equal to the marginal cost of producing it.

(4.11)   MC=P under the assumptions of perfect competition.

PROOF OF THE PARETO EFFICIENCY
OF PERFECT COMPETITION

Recall from Chapter 3 that the basic condition for Pareto optimality in a barter economy is that the (common) marginal rates of substitution between the two goods for the two consumers is equal to the rate of product transformation of the two goods, or

$$(3.2) \qquad MRS_{Y \text{ for } X} = RPT_{Y \text{ for } X}$$

Next, we saw above that

$$(4.3) \qquad P_Y / P_X = MU_Y / MU_X = MRS_{Y \text{ for } X}$$

and

$$(4.10) \qquad RPT_{Y \text{ for } X} = MC_Y / MC_X$$

Combining these equations gives us the proof that Pareto efficiency occurs when:

$$(4.12) \qquad P_Y / P_X = MC_Y / MC_X$$

This is the defining property of a perfectly competitive economy. This result is called the First Fundamental Theorem of Welfare Economics.

The First Fundamental Theorem of Welfare Economics

Given the assumptions of the model of perfect competition, and if all consumers and firms are selfish price takers, a competitive economy must be Pareto efficient.

THE FACTOR MARKET

To complete our discussion of competitive equilibrium we should mention the *factor market*, that is, the demand and supply of factors of production. Using labor as an example, Figure 4.5 illustrates factor demand in a competitive market. The wage rate is set by the forces of supply and demand in the

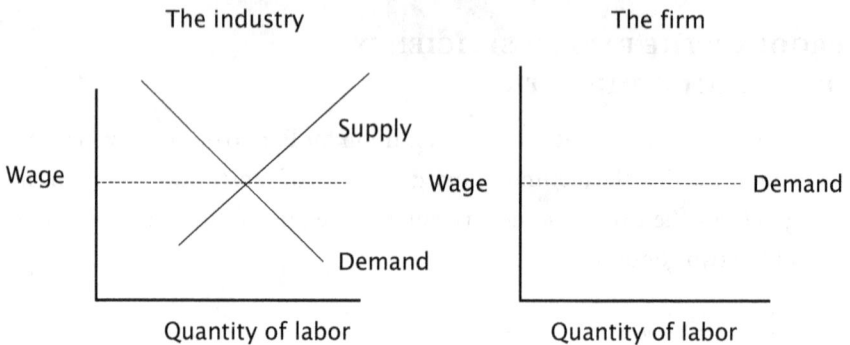

Figure 4.5. Factor demand in a competitive market

labor market for the industry and that wage rate is *given* for the firm. The firm is such a small portion of the industry that it can hire or fire as many workers as it wants to without affecting the wage rate. The demand curve for labor for a firm in a competitive labor market is a horizontal line. In economic jargon, the demand for labor is *perfectly elastic*.

To determine how much of an input a firm will employ, we need two more pieces of information. The demand for a factor of production is a ***derived demand***. It depends not only on the efficiency of the input in producing the good in question, but it also depends on the value of the good being produced. So we need to know the price of the good being produced and the marginal physical product (MPP) of labor (or whatever factor input we are considering). If the marginal physical product of an additional worker is two widgets, and the price of a widget is $5, then the value of the marginal product (VMP) of an additional worker is $10 and that is the equilibrium wage rate. Under conditions of perfect competition in the goods market the price of widgets would be constant at $5. The marginal physical product is declining because of the **law of diminishing returns**. As more and more units of labor are applied to the other fixed inputs, the MPP will eventually decline. So the VMP curve is downward sloping. In equilibrium, we have

(4.13) $\text{VMP} = P_{good} \times \text{MPP}_{factor}$

In equilibrium, the wage is equal to the value of the marginal product. As shown in Figure 4.6, this determines the equilibrium number of workers employed, here labeled Le. Another "law" of factor demand is that, in a competitive factor market, the ratio of the factor prices should equal the ratio of factor marginal products.

This is illustrated in Figure 4.7 with the two factors capital and labor. In this case, output is maximized at the point where the isoquant is just tangent to the *isocost curve* ($C = P_K K + P_L L$). As we saw in Chapter 2, equation (2.4),

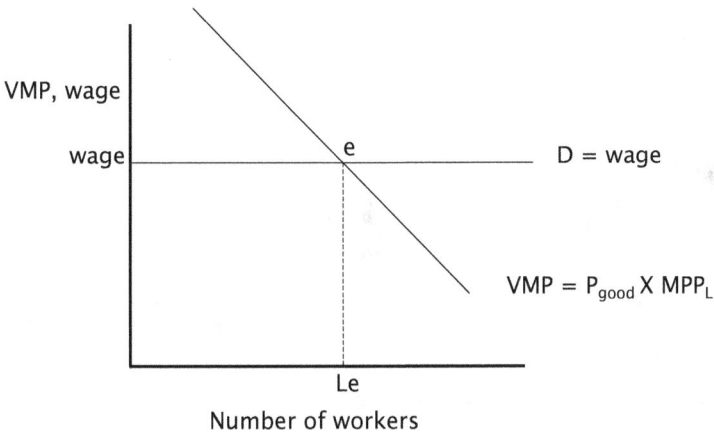

Figure 4.6. The value of the marginal product rule

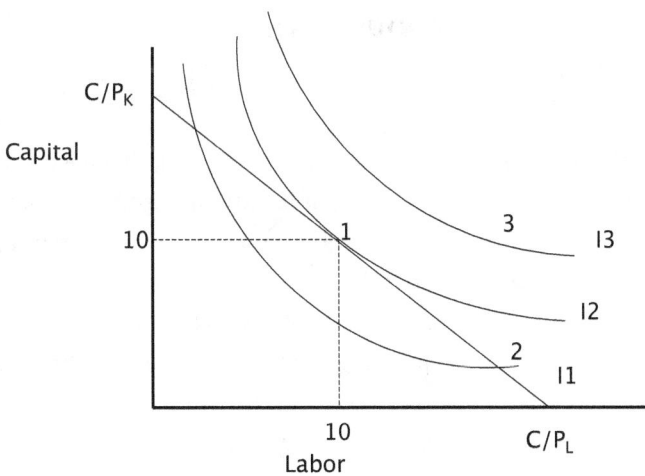

Figure 4.7. Maximizing output subject to a cost constraint

the slope of the isoquant, dK/dL, is equal to the ratio of marginal products MP_L/MP_K. The equation for the isocost curve is $K=C/P_K-(P_L/P_K)L$ and its slope dK/dL is $-P_L/P_K$. So maximizing output given factor cost constraint occurs when

(4.14) $P_L/P_K=MPL/MPK$, or

(4.15) $MPK/P_K=MPL/P_L$

By convention the wage rate P_L is usually denoted by w, and the price of capital, P_K, is usually denoted by r (the rental price of capital).

Prices and the Model of a Barter Economy

According to Walrasian theory, given the same initial conditions, a perfectly competitive economy will achieve the same Pareto efficient outcome as would happen in a face-to-face barter economy. This system places an extraordinary burden on prices to contain all the necessary information about goods and factors of production. A Pareto efficient outcome also depends critically on the ability of consumers and producers to respond rationally and consistently to these price signals.

THE CLARK–WICKSTEED PRODUCT EXHAUSTION THEOREM

In Chapter 2 we saw that under competitive conditions in the long run, factors of production are paid according to their marginal physical products. According to the results of Euler's theorem, equation (2.23), this means that the total output produced is exactly used up if it is distributed to the factors producing that output according to the condition: factor reward=marginal product. This is a *steady-state system*. If the economy is producing only corn, and if the factors of production are paid in corn, then at the end of the production period the amount of corn produced will be exactly used up in factor payments.

When we add prices to our model this means that the factor price will equal the value of the marginal product. But this is true only if this economy is characterized by constant returns to scale. This condition holds under the assumptions of perfect competition, as can be seen in Figure 4.4 showing long-run competitive equilibrium. As shown in the figure, a competitive firm will operate at the minimum point on the long-run average cost curve. To the left of this point the economy is characterized by increasing returns to scale (decreasing unit costs), and to the right of this point it is characterized by decreasing returns to scale (increasing costs). So when the economy is in long-run competitive equilibrium it is characterized by constant returns to scale, and there is no "adding-up" problem. If factors are paid according to the value of their marginal products, then the value of total output is exactly equal to the value of the contributions of the factors of production. This is known as the Clark–Wicksteed product exhaustion theorem, named for its formulators, J. B. Clark and Phillip Wicksteed, in the 1890s.

WALRASIAN ECONOMICS IN PRACTICE

It is easy to see why the Walrasian system has held sway for so long. It is nothing less than a complete and logically consistent (if one accepts all the underlying assumptions) representation of Adam Smith's invisible hand. The mathematical form of the system lends itself to easy statistical tests of different questions about the substitutability of goods and inputs, the efficiency of particular markets, and the rate of technological change. But the validity of applying the Walrasian model depends on critical assumptions about human nature, the physical representation of technology, and the characteristics of particular markets. And contrary to the widely held opinion that all models contain assumptions and therefore the realism of assumptions is irrelevant, these assumptions do matter. The question is whether or not the models of *Homo economicus* and perfect competition can be used to make accurate predictions about real-world market behavior. This is examined in Part Two of this book.

Economists are quick to point out that the field is changing rapidly and that much theoretical work being done today does not accept the basic premises of the Walrasian competitive model. This is true. But the basic tools widely used by economists implicitly incorporate the assumptions of that model. The Walrasian model is still the backbone of contemporary economics. *The*

*major tools of economic analysis are derived from the Walrasian model and the
equilibrium conditions associated with it.* To help understand how the model
works in practice, it is useful at this point to consider some specific applications. Here are some examples.

Price and Income Elasticities

Consumer demand for a good in the Walrasian model is a function of the
prices of available goods and the consumer's income (M=budget). Consider
the demand for good X in the two-good economy:

(4.16) $Q_X = f(P_X, P_Y, M)$

Assume there is no **money illusion**, that is, a proportionate change in all
prices and income will have no effect on the quantities of X and Y purchased.
This is called *homogeneity of degree zero*. In the consumer demand system
described above, all the relevant relationships are in terms of ratios. In Figure
4.1 the intercepts of the budget line are M/P_X and M/P_Y, and the common
slope of the budget line and isoquant is P_Y/P_X. Multiplying all three terms by
some constant does not affect their values.

▶ **ASSUMPTION ALERT!** *Money and the Barter Economy*

  *Two assumptions have the effect of ensuring that a competitive money economy will
  operate in the same fashion as the barter model developed in the first three chapters:*

  1. *All relevant information about a good or an input can be captured by its price.*

  2. *There is no money illusion. A 10 percent increase in the supply of money will re-
     sult in a 10 percent increase in all prices. Relative prices are insensitive to changes
     in the amount of money in circulation.* ◀

By Euler's theorem, homogeneity of degree zero implies:

(4.17) $(\Delta Q_X / \Delta P_X)\, P_X + (\Delta Q_X / \Delta P_Y)\, P_Y + (\Delta Q_X / \Delta M)\, M \equiv 0$

Dividing all the terms on the left-hand side of equation (4.16) by Q_X gives the
own-price elasticity (E_{XX}), the **cross-price elasticity** (E_{XY}), and the **income**

elasticity (E_{XM}). It also reveals the relationship (given the negativity of own-price elasticity):

(4.18) $E_{XX} = E_{XY} + E_{XM}$

The value of the own-price elasticity of a good is equal to the sum of the income elasticity and cross-price elasticities. Restrictions such as equation (4.18) are routinely exploited by economists in econometric work. The assumptions built into these relationships are rarely discussed.

The Elasticity of Substitution

As Chapter 2 showed, the elasticity of substitution measures the ability of an economy to substitute one input for another as the relative values of the marginal products of the inputs change.

(4.19) $\sigma = \Delta(K/L)/(K/L) \div [\Delta(MRTS_{L \text{ for } K}) / MRTS_{L \text{ for } K}]$

Because in competitive equilibrium $MRTS_{L \text{ for } K} = MP_L / MP_K$, the elasticity of substitution is usually written

(4.20) $\sigma = \% \, \Delta(K/L) \div \% \, \Delta[(P_L/P_K)]$

Equating the ratios of marginal products to the ratio of factor prices is justified only if the factor market is in competitive equilibrium. This condition requires perfect competition in the goods market and factor market, constant returns to scale, smooth and continuous isoquants, and the output maximization condition. Measures of the elasticity of substitution are widely used in public policy debates. For example, the degree of substitutability between energy and capital has been the topic of many econometric studies. The effects of the built-in assumptions are seldom considered.

Total Factor Productivity

Total factor productivity (TFP) is an attempt to measure the effect of pure technological change on output growth. It is written as:

(4.21) $\dot{A} = \dot{Q} - a\dot{K} - (1-a)\dot{L}$

A dot over an element in equation (4.21) indicates a rate of growth. The weights a and $(1-a)$ are the product shares of capital and labor. In econometric studies estimating TFP, each input is weighted using its cost share rather than its share of the output of the product (in the case of labor this is wL/C). This approach is valid only under conditions of perfect competition in both the goods and factor markets. Perfect competition implies constant returns to scale, constrained optimization, and the assumptions discussed above (see the discussion of the **dual** below). How these assumptions affect the validity of using cost shares as weights is rarely discussed in TFP studies.

APPENDIX

Constrained Optimization and the Lagrangian Multiplier

Constrained optimization is the maximization (or minimization) of some objective function subject to constraints on the independent variable. Consider the problem of maximizing utility subject to a budget constraint. A specific utility function and budget constraint might be:

(4.22) $U = X_1 X_2 + 4X_2$ subject to the budget constraint $2X_1 + X_2 = 30$

The Lagrangian version of this would be:

(4.23) $Z = X_1 X_2 + 4X_2 + \lambda(30 - 2X_1 - X_2)$

The idea is to make the constraint equal to zero so that we can evaluate the utility function without worrying about constraints. In that case U will be equal to Z. This is where λ comes in. We treat λ as an additional variable, that is, instead of the function $U = f(X_1, X_2)$, we have $Z = f(\lambda, X_1, X_2)$. Then the first-order conditions are:

(4.24) $\partial Z / \partial X_1 = X_2 + 2\lambda = 0$

(4.25) $\partial Z / \partial X_2 = X_1 + \lambda = 0$

(4.26) $\partial Z / \partial \lambda = 30 - 2X_1 - X_2 = 0$

By treating λ as an extra variable and solving the system of equations including it, we can treat the values of Z as if they were free (unconstrained) variables.

Kuhn–Tucker Conditions

The mathematics we used above to describe the Pareto conditions for efficiency in exchange are designed for problems of constrained optimization. For example, we began by deriving the conditions for maximizing utility subject to a given endowment of goods X and Y. The Kuhn–Tucker conditions are a way of writing down the constrained optimization problem when there are non-negativity constraints. For example, in the graphical representation of the consumer maximization problem, it is necessary for the consumer to consume positive amounts of both goods or else we might have a situation illustrated in Figure 4.8.

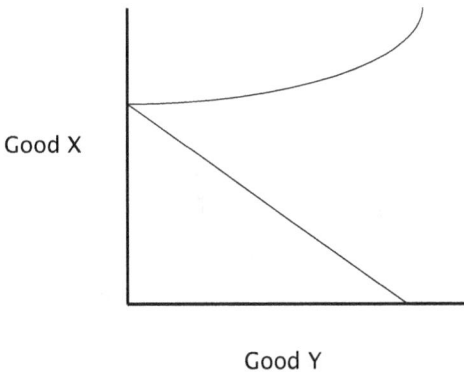

Good X

Good Y

Figure 4.8. A corner solution

In this case the consumer is spending his or her entire budget on good X and it is impossible for the indifference curve to be tangent to the budget line. The consumer's constrained maximization problem becomes:

$$(4.27) \quad Z = U(X, Y) - \lambda(P_X X + P_Y Y - B)$$

$$B \leq P_X X + P_Y Y$$

$$X, Y \geq 0$$

The first-order conditions become:

$$(4.28) \quad \partial Z / \partial X = \partial U / \partial X - \lambda P_X \leq 0 \text{ if } <, \text{ then } X = 0$$

(4.29) $\partial Z / \partial Y = \partial U / \partial Y - \lambda P_Y \leq 0$ if $<$, then $Y = 0$

(4.30) $\partial Z / \partial \lambda = B - P_X X - P_Y Y \geq 0$ if $>$, then $\lambda = 0$

If $X, Y > 0$, then $MU_X = \lambda P_X$ and $MU_Y = \lambda PX$, and $\lambda = MU_X / P_X = MU_Y / P_Y$.

If the total budget is not spent, and there is some income left over after the consumer has all the X and Y desired, then the marginal utility of income λ must be zero.

The Dual and the Function Coefficient

There is an important relationship between cost functions and production functions called the dual. Figure 4.7 shows the conditions for output maximization given a cost constraint. We can arrive at the same result if we start with a production function (an isoquant) and see how we can produce a given amount of output with minimum cost (the lowest isocost curve). We could produce the given output using the quantities of labor and capital indicated by points 1 or 2 on isocost curve I3 (see Figure 4.9), but we can produce it cheaper by using the combination of labor and capital indicated by point e on isocost curve I2. With isocost I1 we do not have enough money to purchase the inputs necessary to produce the quantity of output indicated by the isoquant.

So whether we start with the isoquant and minimize costs, or start with the isocost curve and maximize output, we arrive at the same optimal amounts of inputs K and L. In economic theory this is called the dual. As we saw above,

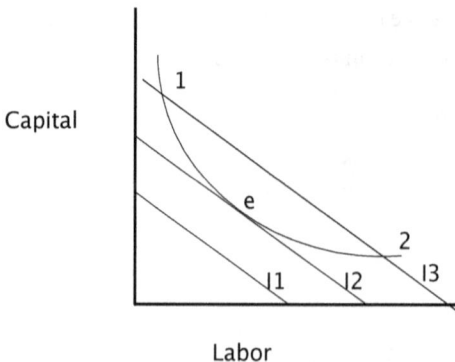

Figure 4.9. Minimizing costs subject to an output constraint

this means that, with competitive equilibrium in production, the slope of the isoquant is tangent to the isocost curve, so that the ratio of factor prices is equal to the ratio of marginal products. This is a particularly important result because, with the equilibrium assumption, it is possible to start with a production function and go directly to a cost function.

The **function coefficient** is the proportional change in output resulting in an equal proportional change in all inputs. Given two inputs K and L and output Q, we have:

(4.31) $\varepsilon = (\Delta Q / Q) / (\Delta K / K) + (\Delta Q / Q) / (\Delta L / L) = (\Delta Q / \Delta K) / (K / Q)$
$+ (\Delta Q / \Delta L) / (L / Q)$, or

(4.32) $\varepsilon = MP_K (K / Q) + MP_L (L / Q)$

Now multiply the first term on the left-hand side by $1 = P_K / P_K$ and the second term by $1 = P_L / P_L$. This gives us:

(4.33) $\varepsilon = (MPK / P_K) (KP_K / Q) + (MPL / P_L) (LP_L / Q)$

We saw above in equation (4.15) that equilibrium in the factor market requires that $(MPK / P_K) = (MPL / P_L)$, so we can rewrite equation 4.33 as

(4.34) $\varepsilon = (MPK / P_K)[(KP_K + LP_L) / Q]$

We saw above that the cost constraint $C = (KP_K + LP_L)$ and we know that C / Q is the average cost of producing a unit of Q, so we can write 4.34 as

(4.35) $\varepsilon = (MPK / P_K)(AC)$

The last thing we need to do is to show that (P_K / MPK) is equal to long-run marginal cost LMC. Suppose we wanted to produce one more unit of Q and that the marginal product of capital is five. How many units of capital would be needed? The answer is 1/5. How much would that cost? The answer is (P_K) $(1 / MPK)$. So the function coefficient can be written as

(4.36) $\varepsilon = LAC / LMC$

We began with a production function and ended up with an expression made up only of costs. We did this by making the critical assumption that the factor market was in competitive equilibrium so that we could convert marginal products to marginal costs. This is critically important in econometric studies because there is no data on marginal products of inputs, but there is data on wages, rent, interest, and other input costs. The graphical result above showing the duality between cost and production can be proved mathematically using *Shephard's Lemma*, an application of a mathematical relationship called the *envelope theorem*.

The Theory of the Second Best

If several optimality conditions in an economic model are not satisfied, would we move toward Pareto efficiency by correcting only one of them? The surprising answer is no. It is not only possible but very likely that correcting one of the imperfections will move us farther away from the competitive ideal. This result is called the theory of the second best, as first demonstrated by R. G. Lipsey and Kevin Lancaster in the 1950s. The very practical policy implication of the theory is that economists need to carefully examine the specific characteristics of a particular market before making theory-based "first-best" recommendations about how to improve economic efficiency. Richard Howarth examined the effects on the economy of environmental taxes and found that first-best rules underestimate the optimal level of emissions taxes under a variety of policy scenarios (see Howarth 2005).

GLOSSARY

Accounting profit—The actual profit a firm makes, that is, the total revenue from selling the goods produced minus the total costs of producing them. Accounting profit does not include opportunity costs.

Cross-price elasticity—The effect of a change in the price of one good on the quantity demand of another. The effect is negative for goods that are complements (i.e., used together, such as gin and tonic) and positive for goods that are substitutes (such as apples and oranges).

Derived demand—The market for a factor of production depends not only on its productivity but also on the demand for the product it is producing.

Dual—Maximizing output subject to a cost constraint or minimizing costs subject to an output constraint gives the same optimal combinations of inputs.

Economic profit—The profit a firm makes minus the average profit prevailing in the economy. In long-run competitive equilibrium, profits and losses are eliminated by the forces of competition so that economic profit is zero for all firms. That means all firms are making the same accounting profit.

First-order conditions—When a consumer is maximizing utility subject to a budget constraint, the ratio of marginal utilities will equal the ratio of the prices of the goods. When a producer is maximizing output subject to a cost constraint, the ratio of the marginal products of the factors of production will equal the ratio of their prices.

Function coefficient—The proportional change in output resulting in an equal proportional change in all inputs.

Income elasticity—The effect of a change in income on the demand for a good. The effect is positive for normal goods (your income goes up so you buy more of it) and negative for inferior goods (your income goes up and you buy less of it).

Kuhn-Tucker conditions—A way of stating the first-order conditions for a constrained optimization problem when there are non-negativity constraints on the variables to be maximized.

Law of demand—The price of a good and the quantity demanded of it are inversely related, or $dQ_d / dP < 0$.

Law of diminishing returns—As more and more units of a productive factor are added, the amounts of all other factors held constant, the marginal physical product of that factor will eventually decline.

Law of supply—The price of a good and the quantity of it supplied are directly related, or $dQ_s / dP > 0$.

Marginal utility of money—When the consumer is maximizing utility subject to a budget constraint, the consumer gets the same utility from a dollar spent on each good. So in equilibrium, $\lambda = MUx / Px = MU_Y / P_Y$ can be interpreted as the marginal utility of money.

Money illusion—The failure to distinguish between nominal (actual) and real (adjusted for inflation) prices.

Opportunity cost—The cost foregone by not choosing the next best alternative. For a firm, it is the profit foregone by not producing in the next most profitable industry.

Own-price elasticity—The effect of an increase in the price of a good on the quantity of it demanded.

Production possibilities frontier—Shows the maximum amount of one good that can be produced, given the amount produced of the other good. On the frontier, resources and technology are used to their maximum efficiency.

Rate of product transformation—The rate at which the resources used in the production of one good can be shifted to the production of another good while maintaining the greatest output efficiency possible. It is equal to the slope of the production possibilities frontier.

Second-order condition—Necessary to ensure that we are obtaining a maximum value and not a minimum value.

REFERENCE

Howarth, R. 2005. The present value criterion and environmental taxation: The suboptimality of first-best decision rules. *Land Economics* 81, 321–336.

MARKET FAILURE AND THE SECOND FUNDAMENTAL THEOREM OF WELFARE ECONOMICS

What is it we mean by "market failure"? Typically, at least in allocation theory, we mean the failure of a more or less idealized system of price-market institutions to sustain "desirable" activities or stop "undesirable" activities. The desirability of an activity, in turn, is evaluated relative to the solution values of some explicit or implied maximum welfare problem.

—*Francis Bator, "The Anatomy of Market Failure,"* Quarterly Journal of Economics *72(3) (1958), 351*

The model of perfect competition presented in the last chapter is the heart and soul of neoclassical welfare economics. It is a mathematical representation of an economic system that exactly duplicates the operation of a voluntary, frictionless, barter economy. As we saw in Chapter 1, the starting point for the model is the individual consumer whose behavior is described by the rational actor model. The consumer chooses from among the array of market goods based solely on the prices of those goods, and producers supply these goods using the most efficient combinations of inputs as indicated by their prices (see Figure 5.1). Two critical assumptions drive the demand for market goods in this model. The first is the assumption of rational choice on the part of consumers and producers, and the second is faith in the ability of prices to correctly capture all the relevant information about market goods. If the price signals are "wrong," then so too will be the collection of market goods chosen by the rational consumer.

The rational actor   **The competitive firm**

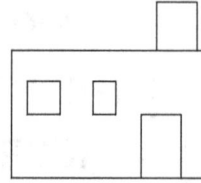

Goods and services

Prices

Stable preferences

More is always preferred to less   Perfect information
Consistency in choices   Mobility of factors
Preferences are stable   No barriers to entry
Responds rationality to price signals   Uses best technology
Every preference is equally valid   Constant returns to scale
No interaction   No interaction

Figure 5.1. Assumptions of the Walrasian model

Much of the criticism of neoclassical economics is centered on the First Fundamental Theorem, namely, a competitive economy will ensure the most efficient allocation of society's resources in consumption and production. It is easy to see that real economies bear little resemblance to the competitive ideal. But this is recognized by neoclassical economics. Sometimes prices are distorted and the market fails to achieve the socially optimal result. Instances of **market failure** include **externalities, public goods,** and **market power.** In all these cases, prices are distorted and there is a legitimate role for the government to intervene and correct the market failures.

EXTERNALITIES

An externality occurs when the action of one economic agent (consumer or firm) affects another agent, and this effect is not included in market prices. When this occurs, the private market price is not equal to the **social price** of the good.

In Figure 5.2, a factory producing some good (perhaps widgets) is emitting air pollution that affects nearby residents. This air pollution might cause health

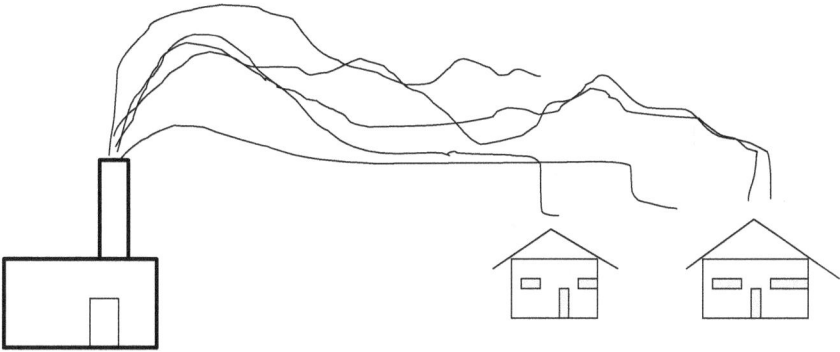

Figure 5.2. An externality in production

damages, extra cleaning costs, or reduced visibility. If these damages are not included in production costs, the "true" (social) cost of producing a widget would be higher than the cost to the (private) producer and thus higher than the market price. This is the case even if all the assumptions of Walrasian theory hold, including perfect competition, the rational actor model, and so on. Figure 5.3 shows the effect of a negative externality on the price and quantity of a good.

If the external costs of production were not accounted for, the (private) price would be set at P_P and the quantity produced would be Q_P. Including the external effects of production would increase the price to P_S (the social price) and decrease the quantity demanded to Q_S. When externalities are present, consumers respond rationally to prices, and prices are capable of containing all relevant information, but the wrong prices are sent to the market. Once these prices are corrected, a socially efficient allocation of resources can be obtained.

Two classic solutions to externalities are (1) the use of taxes and subsidies and (2) completely assigning property rights. Arthur Pigou, writing in the 1920s, argued for a tax on negative externalities such as pollution and subsidies for positive externalities such as beekeeping (which has a positive effect on the production of many crops). Ronald Coase argued that the socially optimal amount of an externality would automatically be arrived at if property rights were assigned to either the polluter or pollutee. In the first case the pollutee would pay the polluter not to pollute, and in the second case the

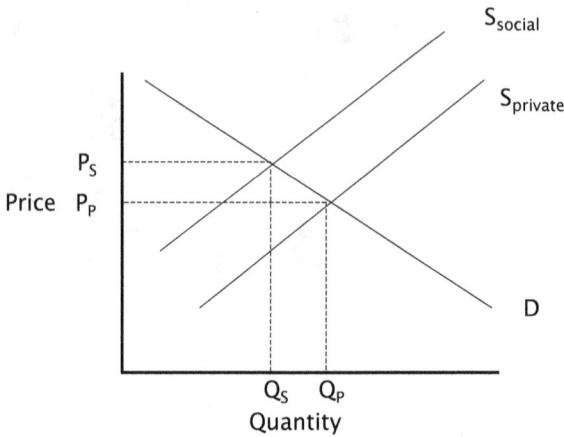

Figure 5.3. Price and quantity of a good associated
with a negative externality

polluter would pay for the right to pollute. No matter to which party property rights are assigned, with perfect information and no transactions costs, the situation would be reached where the marginal cost of pollution would exactly equal the marginal benefit from the polluting activity.

PUBLIC GOODS

Public goods have two characteristics that preclude assigning them a proper price so they can be efficiently allocated.

1. Public goods are non-exclusive. Once a public good is provided, anyone can use it whether or not that person paid for its use.

2. Public goods are non-rival. Once a public good is provided, one person's use does not affect another person's use of that good.

An example of a pure public good is public radio. Once a public radio station is operating, anyone can listen to that station whether or not that person sends in a donation to the station. Also, any number of people can listen to the station without affecting any other person's use. The marginal cost of adding one more person is zero.

Many goods have one of these characteristics and not the other. For example, cable TV is exclusive but not rival. People can be excluded from using it if they do not pay a cable fee, but up to a point more customers can be added without affecting the supply of cable TV services. Other goods are rival but not exclusive. The fishery is a classic example of a good of this sort. If a fishing ground is not regulated by some government or private cooperative, anyone can go there and fish. But, because the number of fish is limited in any given area, if one person catches a fish no one else can catch that fish. The private incentive is to catch the fish before someone else does. This is called the *tragedy of the commons.*

The Tragedy of the Commons

In the case of a finite, open-access resource there is an incentive for each individual to use the resource as quickly as possible before someone else uses it first. One solution to the tragedy is to assign property rights, either to private individuals or to a public entity.

We saw in Chapter 4 that a private good is efficiently provided by the market if its price is equal to its marginal cost. Price is determined by the intersection of demand and supply in the market for that good. In the case of a public good, efficient allocation results when the marginal social value of the good is equal to the marginal cost of providing it. The social benefit of a public good is determined by vertically summing the demand curves for the consumers in the market for that good, as shown in Figure 5.4.

Figure 5.4 shows the usual textbook solution to the public goods problem. The efficient provision of the public good is determined by the point where the public good demand curve (vertical sum of D1+D2) equals the marginal cost of producing the good. So the efficient price would be P_{pg} and the optimal amount provided would be Q_{pg}. This solution is a little disingenuous because for a pure public good, once it exists, the marginal cost of providing it to one more user is zero. In that case, the price would be zero and the optimal amount provided would be Q_{ppg}.

FOUR SHEPHERDS WHO OWN FOUR SHEEP GRAZE TOGETHER...

WHAT WOULD HAPPEN IF I GOT ANOTHER SHEEP?

BENEFIT OF +1...

NEGATIVE OVERGRAZING, OF -1

MUST ADD ANOTHER SHEEP...

TRAGEDY OF THE COMMONS

SHEEP'S RIGHTS YEH.

NO GRASS

ENOUGH FLOCKS

MORE LAND NOW! SHEEP POWER

WOE! WOE!

I CAN SEE LAND

FEED FEEL FREE

GET DOLLY

GARRETT HARDIN WAS RIGHT!

EXTRA SPACE NOW!

FEED ME

Price of the P_{pg} Marginal cost
public good

D1 + D2

D2

D1

Q_{pg} Q_{ppg}
Quantity of the public good

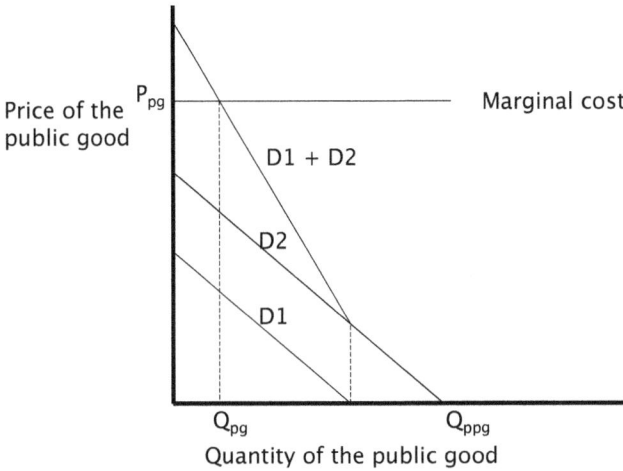

Figure 5.4. The optimal provision of a public good

MARKET POWER

A fundamental characteristic of perfect competition is that firms are price takers; each firm is so small relative to the market that its actions have no effect on price. The price a firm can receive for a good is dictated by the forces of supply and demand in the market for that good. In economic jargon, the firm faces a horizontal, perfectly elastic demand curve. For a monopolist, however, the firm controls the entire market, and so it faces a downward sloping demand curve.

As shown in Figure 5.5, the monopolist faces a downward sloping demand curve, and a marginal cost curve lying under the demand curve. In the case of a linear demand curve, the demand curve (in inverse form) is $P = a + 2Q$ (where a is a constant) and the slope would be $dP/dQ = 2$. Total revenue is the quantity sold times price or $PQ = (a+2Q)Q = aQ + 2Q^2$, and marginal revenue is slope of the TR curve $d(PQ)/dQ$ or $(a+4Q)$, so the intercepts of the demand and marginal revenue curves are the same but the slope of the marginal revenue curve $(dMR/dQ = 4)$ is twice as great. As in the case of perfect competition, the firm will produce where $MC = MR$, and in this case the output will be Q_M. The price is taken from the demand curve and the quantity Q_M is

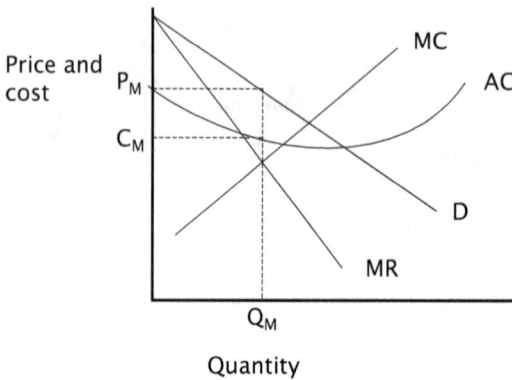

Figure 5.5. Price, output, and average cost under monopoly

associated with a price of P_M. At that quantity the average unit cost of production is C_M, which is less than the price, so the firm makes a profit of $(P_M - C_M)$ Q_M. Unlike the competitive firm, a firm with market power can earn an economic profit, that is, a rate of profit greater than the average rate prevailing in the economy. The monopolistic firm produces at a point other than the minimum on the long-run average cost curve and can control price by changing the quantity sold.

The efficiency of monopoly compared with perfect competition can be seen in Figure 5.6. If the market for the good being produced were competitive, the amount produced would be Qc, determined by the point where the marginal cost curve intersects with the demand curve (the demand curve would represent the sum of the marginal revenue curves for all the producers). The price would be Pc (price=marginal cost=marginal revenue).

In the case of a monopolistic firm, output would be determined where MC=MR, the quantity produced would be Qm, and the price would be Pm. A monopolist produces less and charges more than a firm operating under conditions of perfect competition. In the Walrasian general equilibrium framework, this represents a loss to society because less of this good is being produced than is socially optimal.

The effect of this can be seen using the concept of **consumer surplus**. Under competitive conditions, the price of the good in Figure 5.6 would be Pc.

Looking at the demand curve, if the price were higher than Pc, would there still be some demand for the good? The answer is clearly yes. Some people are willing to pay a higher price than Pc for the good. So they are in a sense receiving a "bonus," or surplus, compared with what they would be willing to pay. Total consumer surplus under competitive conditions in Figure 5.6 is the area of the triangle acPc.

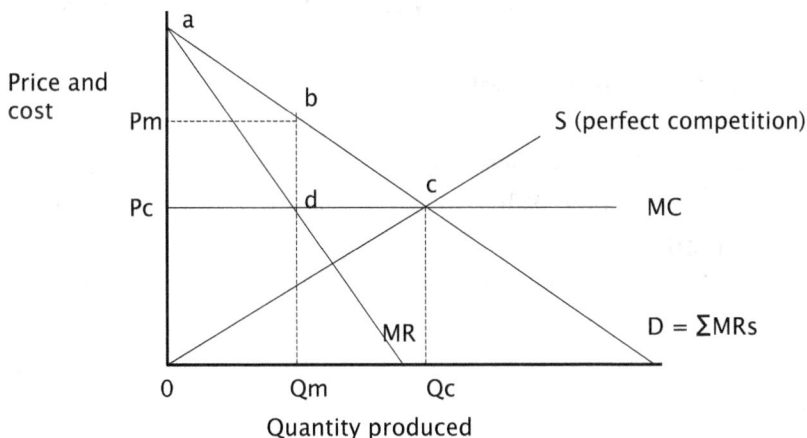

Figure 5.6. The loss of social welfare under monopoly

Looking at Figure 5.6 from the point of view of the producer, we can see that some sellers would be willing to sell the good at a price less than the competitive price of Pc. They too are getting a bonus, and this is called **producer surplus**. In Figure 5.6, under competitive conditions, producer surplus would be the area under the competitive supply curve cOPc.

Suppose this industry were characterized by monopoly power? In that case, the firm would set the price at Pm and consumer surplus would be reduced to the area abPm. Compared with the competitive situation, this represents a loss of consumer surplus equivalent to the area (acPc − abPm) or PcPmbc. But part of this loss goes to the producer as producer surplus (the area PcPmbd). This does not represent a loss to society; it is simply a transfer from consumers to producers. But the area bcd totally disappears. This is called a **deadweight loss** and represents the cost to society of the monopolization of this industry. The rationale for this is that society would prefer that more scarce resources be used to make this good but instead they are going to their next best use (whatever that is).

PRICES AND MARKET FAILURE

In all three classic cases of market failure, the economy fails to achieve general Pareto efficiency because the wrong prices are sent to consumers. When externalities are present, prices do not reflect the "external" effects of production. Because of the free-riding problem, the prices of public goods underestimate their true value to society. Monopolists can control the prices they charge in order to influence the quantity sold. All of these instances of market failure are ubiquitous in real economies. This fact is recognized by most economists. Most economists are not free-market fundamentalists, and they recognize a legitimate role for government intervention to correct market failures. And within the Walrasian system, there is a theoretically tractable way of doing this.

We saw in Chapters 1 (consumption) and 2 (production) that any particular Pareto-efficient outcome depends on the initial distribution of society's resources (goods or productive inputs). So if market failure results in an unsatisfactory outcome from society's point of view, all we have to do is change the initial distribution of resources (a lump-sum transfer) in order to move to the socially desirable outcome. This is perhaps the most important idea for Walrasian economic policy. It is called the Second Fundamental Theorem of Welfare Economics, and it provides the intellectual rationale for policies promoting efficient markets.

The Second Fundamental Theorem of Welfare Economics

Assuming that consumers and producers are rational, self-regarding price takers, almost any Pareto-efficient outcome can be supported by lump-sum transfers.

Broadly interpreted, the Second Fundamental Theorem says that if market imperfections exist, it is possible to correct them through enlightened intervention. It is usually interpreted more narrowly to mean that if an imperfection exists, it is better to address the problem through income transfers rather than by adjusting prices. That is, the best policy is to adjust initial endowments and let the market take over.

For completeness we should also mention the Third Fundamental Theorem of Welfare Economics, the Arrow impossibility theorem.

The Third Fundamental Theorem of Welfare Economics

This is simply the Arrow impossibility theorem. There is no social welfare function that satisfies Arrow's criteria of universality, non-dictatorship, Pareto efficiency, and independence.

The power of neoclassical welfare economics comes directly from the First and Second Welfare Theorems. These theorems are nothing short of the intellectual foundation for arguments for the efficacy of free-market economies in achieving the highest possible social welfare. Of course, if these theorems are shown to be invalid it does not automatically throw out the case for market allocation of society's scarce resources. But it does call into question market efficiency as a universal first principle of resource allocation. If these theorems do not hold, the case for free markets must be based on specific evidence and the specific conditions of particular situations. This is, in fact, the current trend in economic research and policy. There is a growing recognition of the theoretical intractabilities and the behavioral limitations of Walrasian welfare economics. This is the subject of Part Two of this book.

APPENDIX

Income and Substitution Effects

A fundamental principle of economics is the **law of demand**. All other things being equal, the price of something and the quantity demanded of it are inversely related, or in mathematical notation, $dQ/dP < 0$. There are two reasons for this relationship. First, if the price of a good increases, then the consumer's **real income** (income adjusted for inflation) will decline; and if the good is a **normal good** ($dQ/dI > 0$), then fewer units of that good will be demanded. This is called the **income effect**. Second, an increase in the price of one good (X in this case) relative to another ($[Px/Py]\uparrow$) will cause consumers to substitute good X for good Y. This is the **substitution effect**.

Accounting for the loss of real income affects the demand curve. The ordinary, or **Marshallian demand curve**, named for Alfred Marshall, shows both the income and substitution effects. The **Hicksian demand curve**, named from John Hicks, is *income compensated*, that is, the consumer is compensated for increases or decreases in real income as prices change. In Figure 5.7 notice that the Hicksian demand curve is steeper, less elastic (less price-responsive) compared with the ordinary market demand curve. This is because part of the response to a price change has been taken away.

It is straightforward to show how these effects can be separated using graphs or mathematics. Figure 5.8 is a graphical representation of the income and substitution effects. Suppose there is a price increase in good Y from P_Y' to P_Y. This shifts the budget line inward because at the higher price the consumer can buy less of good Y with his fixed budget M. The optimal amount of good Y purchased at price P_Y' is Y3, where the indifference curve I2 is just tangent to the original budget line at point c. The optimal amount of good Y purchased at price P_Y is Y1, where indifference curve I1 is just tangent to the new budget line at point a.

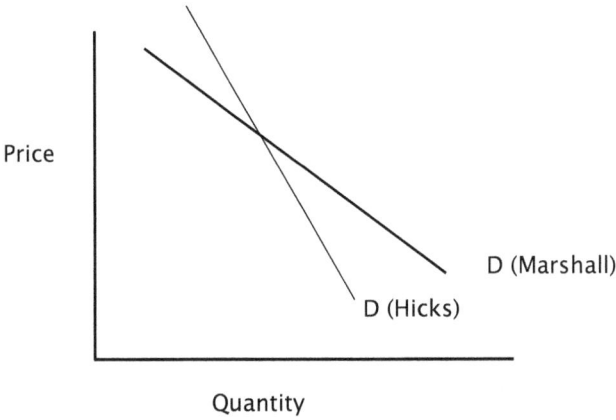

Figure 5.7. Demand according to Hicks and Marshall

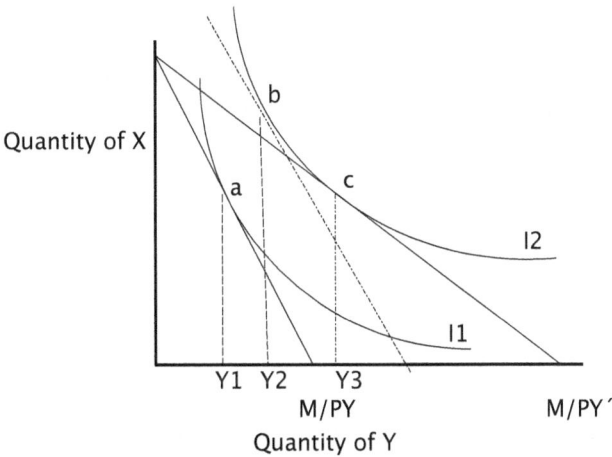

Figure 5.8. Income and substitution effects for a price
increase in a normal good

We can separate the income and substitution effects by giving the consumer enough income so that the consumer can be back on the original indifference curve I2. This is shown by the dotted budget line that is just tangent to
the indifference curve I2 at point b. So we have compensated the consumer for
a loss of real income due to the price increase in good Y by giving the consumer

enough money to move back to the original indifference curve. When the price of Y went up, the total effect was to reduce the amount of Y purchased from Y3 to Y1 (the movement from c to a in Figure 5.8). The movement from Y3 to Y2 (c to b along the original indifference curve) is the substitution effect. The movement from Y2 to Y1 (b to a) is the income effect.

The total effect of a price change is always negative (the law of demand), $P_Y \uparrow Q_Y \downarrow$. The substitution effect is also always negative, $(P_Y / P_X) \uparrow Q_Y \downarrow$. As the price of good Y increases relative to the price of good X, a consumer will substitute good X for good Y. In the case of a normal good the income effect is also negative, $P \uparrow M \downarrow Q_Y \downarrow$. For an **inferior good,** however, the income effect is positive, $P \uparrow M \downarrow Q_Y \uparrow$, partially (but not entirely) offsetting the negative substitution effect.

Mathematically, this result can be derived using a variety of approaches. An interesting interpretation of the income and substitution effects is given by the *Slutsky equation*, named for the early twentieth-century mathematician Eugen Slutsky. Stated in words, the Slutsky equation shows that the slope of the ordinary (Marshallian) demand curve for some good X is equal to the slope of the income-compensated (Hicksian) demand curve minus the optimal amount of good X purchased times the slope of the **Engel curve.** The Engel curve shows the change in the amount of a good (X) purchased resulting from a change in income (dX / dM) keeping prices constant. In elasticity form the Slutsky equation is:

$$(5.1) \qquad E_{11} = E_{11 \text{ (utility held constant)}} - \alpha_1 E_{1M}$$

The own-price elasticity (E_{11}) is equal to the substitution effect (the income-compensated own-price elasticity) minus the income elasticity (E_{1M}) times the budget share of the good ($\alpha_1 = P_1 Q_1 / M$).

The relationships in equation (5.1) implies that the Hicksian and Marshallian measures should be about the same either if the budget share of the good is small or if demand for the good is relatively insensitive to income changes. This is an important point because if the term $\alpha_1 E_{1M}$ is near zero, we can use the market demand curve (and market data directly) for estimates of welfare changes. The three measures of consumer surplus should be about the same. How much people are willing to pay for a gain (WTP) should be about the same as how much they would have to be compensated to accept a similar loss (WTA).

Consumer Surplus According to Hicks and Marshall

The two different kinds of demand curves, ordinary and income-compensated, yield different measures of consumer surplus. Figure 5.9 shows the effect on consumer surplus of a price change for a good. The curve labeled D_M is the Marshallian (ordinary or market) demand curve. Consumer surplus is the area $A+B$ under this demand curve corresponding to the two different prices. In this case the effect on consumer surplus of a price increase, $-(A+B)$, or price decrease $+(A+B)$ is the same.

In the case of the Hicksian demand curve we get different measures of consumer surplus depending on the direction of the price change. This is because, at a higher price (P1 in Figure 5.9), the consumer has a lower real income, and at a lower price (P2), the consumer has a higher real income. The relevant Hicksian demand curve for price P1 is H1 (lower real income), and

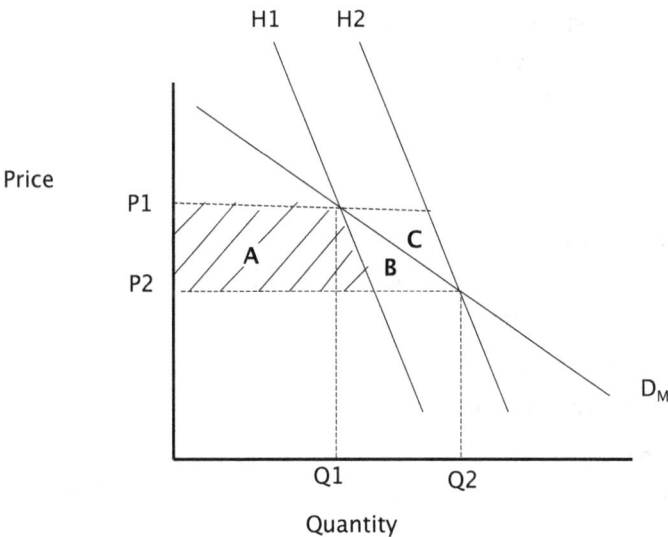

Figure 5.9. Consumer surplus according to Hicks and Marshall

the Hicksian demand curve for price P2 is H2 (higher real income). The gain in consumer surplus resulting from a price move from P1 to P2 is the area under H1, or A. This is called the **compensating variation**. The loss in consumer surplus resulting from a price increase from P2 to P1 is the area under the Hicksian demand curve H2, or A+B+C. This is called the **equivalent variation**.

A=compensating variation

A+B=consumer surplus

A+B+C=equivalent variation

Referring to equation (5.1), the differences between these three measures disappear as the expression $(-\alpha_1 E_{1M})$ becomes smaller.

This discussion of consumer surplus may seem esoteric but it is critically important to **cost-benefit analysis**, one of the basic tools of economics. Traditional cost-benefit analysis relies on Marshallian measures of consumer surplus and they assume that WTA and WTP are similar. As Chapter 8 shows, empirical studies reveal very large differences between the two measures. People are loss averse; they are much less willing to accept losses than they are willing to pay for equivalent gains. This has important consequences for cost-benefit analysis and public policy.

GLOSSARY

Compensating variation—A measure of the welfare gain resulting from a decrease in the price of a good or service. It is equal to the loss in income that would exactly offset the welfare gain from the fall in price.

Consumer surplus—The difference between what consumers actually pay for a good and the extra amount they would be willing to pay.

Cost-benefit analysis—Calculating the benefits and costs of public policies based on identifying potential Pareto improvements. Also called benefit-cost analysis.

Deadweight loss—The net loss of consumer surplus plus producer surplus.

Engel curve—The change in the amount of a good (X) purchased resulting from a change in income (dX/dM), keeping prices constant.

Equivalent variation—A measure of the welfare loss resulting from an increase in the price of a good or service. It is equal to the gain in income that would exactly offset the welfare loss from the price increase.

Externalities—An effect from production or consumption that is not taken account of by market prices. An externality may be either positive or negative.

Hicksian demand curve—A demand curve that includes only changes in relative prices of the good. Also called an income-compensated demand curve.

Income effect—The effect on consumption of a gain or loss in real income.

Inferior good—A good for which an increase in income decreases the demand for it.

Law of demand—The quantity demanded of a good varies inversely with changes in its price.

Market failure—The failure of the market to send "correct" price signals to consumers and firms. Instances include externalities, public goods, and market power.

Market power—The ability of a firm to affect prices and output in a particular market.

Marshallian demand curve—A demand curve that includes the effects of both changes in real income and changes in price. Also called an ordinary demand curve.

Normal good—A good for which an increase in income increases the demand for it.

Producer surplus—The difference between the price sellers actually get for a product and the (lower) price they would be willing to accept.

Public goods—Goods with the characteristics of being non-rival and non-exclusive.

Social price—The price of a good that includes all positive and negative external effects of producing or consuming it.

Substitution effect—The change in the demand for a good arising solely from a change in relative prices, holding utility (usually measured by real income) constant.

PART TWO

MODERN WELFARE ECONOMICS

INTRODUCTION AND OVERVIEW

Part One of this book presents the core framework of Walrasian welfare economics. Its two key ideas are (1) the system was formalized as a theory of exchange in a pure barter economy—prices are added on more or less as an afterthought, and (2) the key assumption that holds the system together is the independent rational actor. Part One is a presentation of standard economic theory, a theory than has been around more or less in its present form for fifty years or more. There is no need for extensive footnotes and references in Part One because the material is presented in dozens of microeconomic textbooks, although not as a logical progression from barter to prices to the fundamental theorems. The material presented in Part One is consistent with other contemporary microeconomic texts, although the behavioral aspects of microeconomic theory are given more emphasis to prepare for the discussion in Part Two.

Part Two presents the modern critique of Walrasian economics from two perspectives. Chapter 6 presents some of the theoretical intractabilities inherent within the mathematical and logical framework of the system. Chapter 7 presents some of the challenges to standard theory from the emerging fields of behavioral economics, evolutionary game theory, and neuroscience. Chapter 8 brings the theoretical and behavioral critiques together in a discussion of cost-benefit analysis and how it is used in contemporary economic analysis of climate change. These critiques set the stage for new directions in economic theory and policy outlined in Chapter 9. The main difference in the presentation of these chapters is the extensive use of references. Most of this material is relatively new, and it is only beginning to appear in introductory economic and microeconomic texts. Another reason for so many references is that many of the new findings in behavioral economics are being published outside the mainstream economic journals. Behavioral economics, evolutionary economics, and neuroeconomics are by their very nature interdisciplinary and experimental, and results are as likely to be published in psychology or biology journals (and the general science journals *Science* and *Nature*) as in the usual economic outlets.

After reading these chapters, it will become clear that the new direction economics will take in the years to come is far from settled. How much of the old economics can be salvaged, how the new behavioral assumptions will coalesce, and the nature of the policy implications of all this are being hammered out at conferences, in online exchanges, and in the pages of leading economic journals. This is an exciting time to study economics. It is hoped that these chapters will not bring uneasiness about the demise of the old but rather optimism about the emergence of economics as an empirically sound and policy-relevant science.

FURTHER READING

Detailed references are provided at the end of the following chapters. Good books and articles to get started on the topics of Part Two include the following:

Critiques of Welfare Theory
Albert, M., and R. Hahnel. 1990. *A Quiet Revolution in Welfare Economics.* Princeton, NJ: Princeton University Press.

Bowles, S., and H. Gintis. 2000. Walrasian economics in retrospect. *Quarterly Journal of Economics* 115, 1411–1439.

Koning, N., and R. Jongeneel. 1997. Neo-Paretian welfare economics: Misconceptions and abuses. Wageningen Economic Papers, 05-97, Wageningen University, The Netherlands.

Mirowski, P. 1989. *More Heat than Light*. Cambridge: Cambridge University Press.

Behavioral Economics, Neuroscience, and Game Theory

Camerer, C., G. Loewenstein, and M. Rabin (eds.). 2004. *Advances in Behavioral Economics*. Princeton, NJ: Princeton University Press.

Gintis, H. 2000. *Game Theory Evolving*. Princeton, NJ: Princeton University Press.

Glimcher, P., M. Dorris, and H. Bayer. 2005. Physiological utility theory and the neuroeconomics of choice. *Games and Economic Behavior* 52, 213–256.

Cost-Benefit Analysis

Ecological Economics, September 2007. Special issue on Benefit-Cost Analysis and Sustainability.

Hanley, N., and C. Spash. 1993. *Cost-Benefit Analysis and the Environment*. Cheltenham, UK: Edward Elgar.

Knetsch, J. 2005. Gains, losses, and the US-EPA *Economic Analyses Guidelines*: A hazardous product. *Environmental & Resource Economics* 32, 91–112.

Pearce, D., G. Atkinson, and S. Mourato. 2006. *Cost-Benefit Analysis and the Environment*. Paris: OECD.

Climate Change

Spash, C. 2002. *Greenhouse Economics*. London: Routledge.

Stern, N. 2007. *The Economics of Climate Change: The Stern Review*. Cambridge: Cambridge University Press.

Happiness and Well-Being

Frey, B., and A. Stutzer. 2002. *Happiness and Economics: How the Economy and Institutions Affect Well-Being*. Princeton, NJ: Princeton University Press.

Layard, R. 2005. *Happiness: Lessons from a New Science*. New York: Penguin.

6

THE THEORETICAL CRITIQUE OF
WALRASIAN WELFARE ECONOMICS

It is the first welfare theorem [asserting the efficiency of competitive
markets] that provides the intellectual foundation for our belief in
market economies. Like any theorem its conclusions depend on the
validity of its assumptions. A closer look at those assumptions,
however, suggests that the theorem is of little relevance to modern
industrial economies.

—*Joseph Stiglitz*, Whither Socialism? *(Cambridge, MA: MIT Press, 1994), 28*

THE IMPORTANCE OF THE FUNDAMENTAL THEOREMS

The foundation for Walrasian economic theory is the two welfare theorems
discussed in chapters 4 and 5. The First Fundamental Theorem states that if
all individuals and firms are selfish price takers, then a competitive equilibrium is Pareto efficient. The Second Fundamental Theorem states that if all
individuals and producers are selfish price takers, then almost any Pareto optimal equilibrium can be supported via the competitive mechanism, provided appropriate lump-sum taxes and transfers are imposed on individuals
and firms.

These two theorems have been the backbone of economic policy in the decades since World War II. Lockwood (1987, 811) writes of the second theorem: "It is no exaggeration to say that the entire modern microeconomic
theory of government policy intervention in the economy (including cost-benefit

This chapter was originally published in a somewhat different form in John M. Gowdy, "The Revolu-
tion in Welfare Economics and Its Implications for Environmental Valuation and Policy," *Land
Economics* 80(2) (2004), 239–257. © 2004 by the Board of Regents of the University of Wisconsin
System. Reproduced by the permission of the University of Wisconsin Press.

analysis) is predicated on this idea." Likewise, Fisher (1983) writes: "The central theorems of welfare economics (i.e. the first and second fundamental theorems) may be the single most important set of ideas that economists have to convey to lay people."

The second theorem implies that if a move from one particular state of the economy to another is judged to be desirable, this move may be achieved through transferring resources from one person (or one activity) to another. Referring back to Chapter 1, any point on the contract curve in Figure 1.3 can be reached by changing the initial distribution of the goods X and Y among the two consumers. The rationale for moving from one state of the economy to another is the Kaldor–Hicks criterion, that is, identifying a potential Pareto improvement (PPI). If the magnitude of the gains from moving from one state of the economy to another is greater than the magnitude of the losses, then social welfare is increased by making the move even if no actual compensation is made. Stavins, Wagner, and Wagner (2002, 5) write about the potential Pareto improvement: "This is the fundamental foundation—the normative justification—for employing benefit-costs analysis, that is, for searching for policies that maximize the positive differences between benefits and costs."

Establishing economic policies using cost-benefit analysis to identify PPIs is one of the central concerns of contemporary economics. A PPI is fundamentally different from the notion of Pareto efficiency that simply says that an efficient state is one in which any change will make at least one person worse

off. A PPI is a change that helps one person and harms another. PPIs are identified using the measures of consumer surplus discussed in Chapter 5.

Two problems mar the welfare-based cost-benefit approach to economic policy. The first is the intractable theoretical difficulty of determining PPIs using the Kaldor–Hicks criterion. This is discussed in this chapter. The second problem is the characterization of human behavior to fit the restrictive assumptions of consumer choice theory. This is discussed in Chapter 7.

What follows is *not* a critique of all attempts to quantify the benefits and costs of moving from one state of the economy to another. Problems arise to the extent that estimates of costs and benefits are shoehorned into the narrow framework of Walrasian theory. Many economists do not appreciate the theoretical difficulties involved in estimating welfare changes. And certainly most non-economists are unaware of the leap of faith required to move from estimating costs and benefits to calculating a potential Pareto improvement.

A Summary of the Walrasian System

1. The theoretical foundation for the policy recommendations of Walrasian economics is the first two theorems of welfare economics.

2. The First Fundamental Theorem justifies relying on a competitive economy to ensure the social good.

3. The Second Fundamental Theorem justifies interventionist policies but only to create the conditions for competitive markets.

4. The system of equations supporting these theorems depends critically on the assumptions about consumer behavior (*Homo economicus*) and the characterization of markets and technology (perfect competition).

5. In this system, policy recommendations are based on the ability to identify efficiency gains (potential Pareto improvements).

6. The ultimate goal of this system is to create a *positive* science of economics, one that can provide policy recommendations without making value judgments, that is, without making interpersonal comparisons of utility.

THEORETICAL INTRACTABILITIES WITH IDENTIFYING POTENTIAL PARETO IMPROVEMENTS

The Kaldor–Hicks criterion seems straightforward. If one person values his or her gains from an economic change more than a second person values his or her losses, then potential total welfare increases, and this represents a potential Pareto improvement. Such an economic change is justified on efficiency grounds even if no actual compensation is paid. In general, economists follow Kaldor's view that economic policy recommendations should be determined by efficiency; distribution is a problem for politicians. Undermining the argument for separating efficiency and distribution is more than sixty years of theoretical work demonstrating that PPIs cannot be identified by comparing individual welfare changes. The goal of economists for most of the last century was to make economics a "positive" science, and the focus on efficiency was supposed to accomplish this. Finding efficiency improvements was supposed to allow economists to avoid interpersonal comparisons of utility. This proved to be an impossible task. The problem in applying the potential Pareto principle is that we are drawing **general equilibrium** conclusions from **partial equilibrium** situations. Partial equilibrium analysis assumes that changes in a particular market can be analyzed independently from all other markets. This is a useful assumption in some practical policy applications of economic theory but is not valid if one is trying to establish the conditions for a general economic optimum. This point is illustrated by the following paradoxes in welfare theory. These paradoxes are particularly debilitating to Walrasian theory because they show that even if we accept all the basic assumptions about economic man and perfectly competitive markets, the theory is still internally inconsistent.

The Cycling Paradox

The PPI criterion was supposed to allow economists to make policy recommendations regarding any two points on different utility possibilities curves such as those shown in Figure 3.4 in Chapter 3. Theoretical difficulties were raised immediately after Kaldor and Hicks proposed in 1939 that identifying PPIs should be the goal of economics. In 1941, Tibor Scitovsky demonstrated

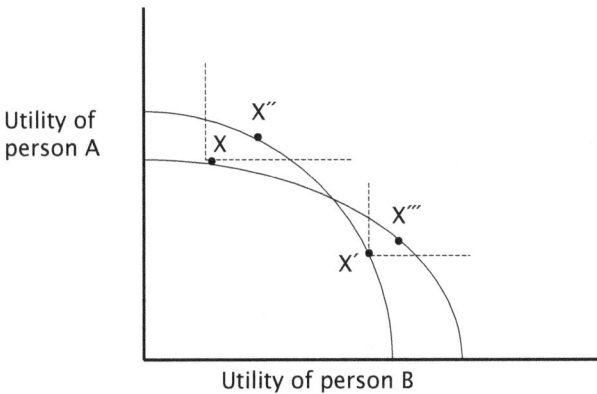

Figure 6.1. The cycling paradox (adapted from Varian 1992, 406)

that if a movement from one point to another in utility space can be shown to be Pareto improving according to the Kaldor–Hicks criterion, then it may also be shown that a movement back to the original point is also Pareto improving. This is sometimes called the cycling paradox. Referring to Figure 6.1, using the PPI criterion a movement from point X to point X′ should be made because from X′ it is possible to move to X″ where both consumers are better off compared with the original point X. It is also true, however, that a movement from X′ to X is justified because from X it is possible to move to point X‴ where both consumers are better off compared with the starting point X′.

To eliminate this cycling problem, Scitovsky proposed a double criterion for a potential Pareto improvement. It must be shown that the gainers from a change can compensate the losers so they will agree to the change (Kaldor criterion) and that it is not possible for the losers to bribe the gainers not to make the move (Hicks criterion). But Gorman (1955) showed that the Scitovsky criterion violates the assumption of transitivity, which as we saw in Chapter 1 is a necessary condition for consistency in consumer choice.

The "Sticking" Paradox
The PPI was one attempt to broaden the Pareto criterion without making interpersonal comparisons of utility. Another attempt, discussed in Chapter 3,

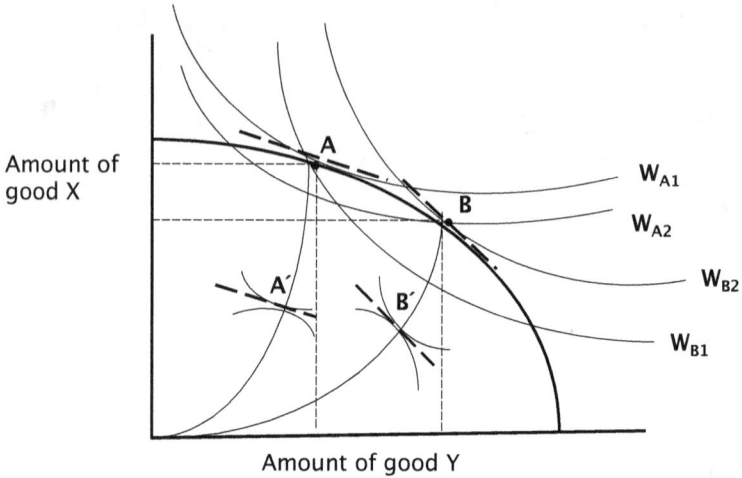

Figure 6.2. A production possibilities frontier with two social welfare optima

was constructing a social welfare function (SWF) to choose a point on a grand utilities possibilities frontier or on a production possibilities frontier (PPF). Figure 6.2 shows that using a SWF might "stick" the choice at either A or B, depending on which was the starting point. If the initial Pareto equilibrium is at B with associated social welfare functions W_{B1} and W_{B2}, point B would be preferred to point A because it is on a higher social welfare curve. However, if the starting point is A with its associated social welfare curves W_{A1} and W_{A2}, then point A would be preferred to point B.

The problem is that any change in initial distribution of goods (income) means a change in the reference points that determine Pareto optimality. The points A and B on the production possibilities frontier are associated with points A′ and B′ within an Edgeworth box for each amount of goods X and Y. Each utility possibilities frontier in Figure 6.2 can be derived from one of the two contract curves for consumption. As we saw in Chapter 3, the necessary condition for general Pareto optimality is that the slope of the production possibilities frontier, the rate of product transformation of Y into X ($RPT_{Y \text{ for } X}$), is equal to the common marginal rates of substitution Y for X ($MRS_{Y \text{ for } X}$) in consumption for each person. These slopes will be different at different points along the PPF, meaning that in competitive equilibrium, the price ratios for X and Y will be different at points A and B. This general interdependence of welfare distributions and relative prices means that we cannot make general equilibrium statements comparing points on the PPF.

The Boadway Paradox

Comparisons of the relative efficiencies of different economic situations depend on identifying gains in consumer surplus (or compensating variations and equivalent variations—CVs and EVs) as discussed in Chapter 5. According to standard cost-benefit practice when comparing different projects or policies, judging which one is superior is a matter of finding the one with the largest net gain. In the 1970s, Robin Boadway (1974) demonstrated that when comparing alternatives, the one with the highest net gain is not necessarily the "best" one as judged by the Kaldor–Hicks compensation test. This is referred to as the Boadway paradox, and it also arises from the fact that estimates of income-compensated variations—welfare gains at constant prices—are partial equilibrium measures. If relative prices change with a redistribution of income, as they almost certainly would in a general equilibrium system, then such estimates are misleading measures of potential welfare gains. These measures coincide with general equilibrium measures only if there is a single market-clearing price ratio at every point on the contract curve, a condition that holds only if preferences are identical and homothetic.

Homothetic Utility Functions

The assumption of "homothenicity" is critical to the Walrasian system and is worth going into in some detail. A homothetic utility function means that the utility maximizing composition of consumption goods depends only on the relative prices of the goods, not income, as shown in Figure 6.3.

A line drawn from the origin (the expansion path of consumption as income increases) will cross the tangency points of the budget lines and indifference curves where these have the same slopes for all levels of income. This means that the marginal rate of substitution between the two goods does not change as income increases. Put another way, the equilibrium (utility maximizing) proportion of all goods consumed remains exactly the same as

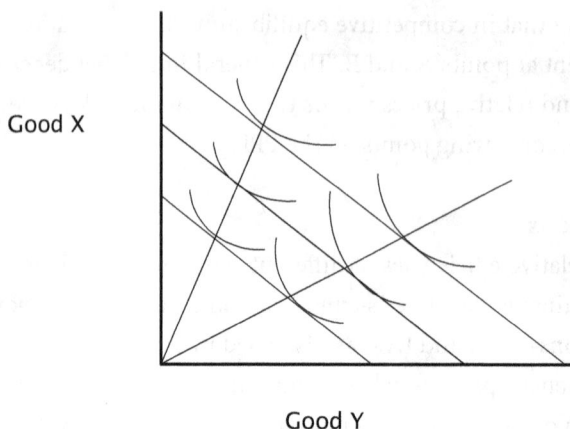

Good X

Good Y

Figure 6.3. Expansion paths for homothetic utility functions

income increases. This is an extremely restrictive and unrealistic assumption. The relative amounts of goods X and Y chosen in Figure 6.3 depend solely on their relative prices. Homothetic utility functions exhibit income elasticities of demand equal to one for all goods for all levels of income. For the whole economy this means that consumers with different incomes but facing the same set of relative prices (as under perfect competition) will demand goods in the same proportions.

Homothenicity is an extremely unrealistic assumption, even in the context of neoclassical economics, but it is necessary to save the Walrasian system and avoid the above paradoxes. Remember that the critical assumption underlying the mathematical properties of consumption and production theory is that there is no interaction between agents. With the homothenicity assumption, everyone has the same preferences and identical marginal utilities of income. An increase in income for the richest person on the planet and the poorest would result in the same proportionate increase in the commodities they consume. People would have identical tastes (utility functions) and there would be no reason to trade goods. The necessity of the homothenicity assumption is one reason why economists resort to the notion of a "representative agent." This is the common theoretical practice of using a single individual to serve as a proxy for all consumers or all firms. The assumption of homothetic preferences, and identical preferences, is obviously a gross violation of reality that must have profound effects on the results of empirical analyses. But it is necessary given the mathematical requirements of Walrasian economics.

A final irony here is worth mentioning. Recall that the goal of **positive economics** is to avoid interpersonal comparisons of utility. But the assumption that utility functions are homogeneous and that the marginal utility of income is the same for all consumers cannot be made without making interpersonal comparisons of utility.

More Problems with PPIs
Numerous other theoretical dilemmas with the PPI approach have been identified. Kjell Brekke (1997) showed that the choice of a numeraire matters when the marginal rates of substitution differ among consumers. Samuelson (1950) showed that it is not certain that group A is better off than group B even if group A has more of everything. Again, a basic problem for welfare economics is that the axioms of consumer choice refer to a single individual and they break down in the case of two or more persons. In the case of two or more persons, even within the narrow framework of neoclassical welfare theory, it cannot even be proved that more is preferred to less—perhaps *the* basic assumption of modern economics (Bromley 1990).

The upshot of these results for welfare economics is that the Kaldor–Hicks PPI rationale for comparing two states of the economy has some fundamental problems that makes it unacceptable as a theoretical foundation for analyzing the costs and benefits of economic policies. There is no theoretically justifiable way to make welfare judgments without invoking value judgments and interpersonal comparisons of utility, yet this is not permissible under the stringent requirements of neoclassical welfare economics. Chipman and Moore (1978, 581) summarized the outcome of discussions about the Kaldor–Hicks–Samuelson–Scitovsky new welfare economics: "After 35 years of technical discussions, we are forced to come back to Robbins' 1932 position. We cannot make policy recommendations except on the basis of value judgments, and these value judgments should be made explicit." This position is even more secure after another twenty-five years of theoretical discussions.

Efficiency, Output Mix, and Social Welfare

As shown in Figure 6.4, it is quite possible that an increase in "efficiency" can reduce social welfare if the output mix changes even if total output increases. Suppose a technological improvement, indicated by an outward shift in the production possibilities frontier, moves the economy from point B to point A on a higher PPF. If we assume that total welfare increases with total consumption, this move should be made under the Kaldor–Hicks test because total consumption (output) goes up. But social welfare declines as indicated by the move from the social welfare function W_3 to a lower social welfare function W_2. In economic arguments for growth, the separability principle is extended to say that the output mix is a political and not an economic problem. It is claimed that efficiency is a "positive" goal, and the question of the mix of goods and productive inputs involves "normative" judgments. An increase in efficiency is a good thing because it is theoretically possible for political authorities to redistribute the efficiency gains so that we could end up at point C on the higher social welfare curve W_4. In practice, the drive for efficiency almost al-

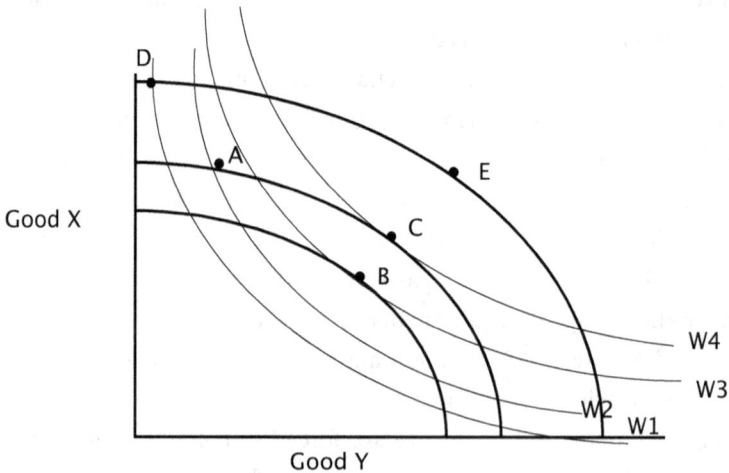

Figure 6.4. Efficiency and social welfare: Efficiency trumps equity

ways overrides equity. Applying the efficiency rule would dictate a move from point A not to point C but rather to point D on a higher PPF but an even lower social welfare curve W_1. Output mix as well as income distribution, both ignored by the PPI criterion, are essential elements of social welfare.

WHY IS THE THEORETICAL CRITIQUE IMPORTANT?

A common defense of Walrasian microeconomics goes something like this: "Of course we know all this. No one really believes that the **real economy** is characterized by the general equilibrium model we use to describe it. But it is good enough." But this model is *the* intellectual foundation for free market policies. If it can be shown that the mathematical logic of the model does not support the fundamental theorems, then there is a crisis of confidence problem for microeconomic theory. If we are no longer sure that the theoretical system generates a Pareto efficient outcome, what does this say about actual markets? Without the Walrasian core to appeal to, economic policies have to be argued case by case with hard empirical evidence about actual costs and benefits. It is no longer enough to set markets in motion and say that a socially optimal outcome will *automatically* be the result.

Exercise

Almost every introductory economic textbook has a discussion about the inefficiency of a minimum wage for workers.

1. Find such a discussion and list the underlying assumptions.

2. Go to an economic literature search engine (or simply Google "minimum wage") and classify the articles (or blogs) according to whether they are for or against a minimum wage.

3. Categorize the groups as to whether they are based on empirical evidence or on Walrasian theory.

IS THE GOAL OF ECONOMIC EFFICIENCY "SCIENTIFIC" OR IS IT AN "IDEOLOGY"?

The policy effect of the development of the various currents and concepts discussed in chapters 1–5 was to focus economics on the concept of efficiency.

In the decades after World War II the job of policy-oriented economists became one of identifying market imperfections, or, in the language of some, finding "money on the table." If resources could be diverted from one use to another and increase total welfare (that is, total economic output), then everyone could (potentially) be better off. This was the job of cost-benefit analysis, and it seemed to finally cast economics as a positive, value-free science. But, as we have seen in this chapter, the theoretical justification for identifying efficiency improvements, the potential Pareto improvement, foundered on theoretical intractabilities. Economic efficiency can no longer claim to be an objective policy criterion.

Daniel Bromley (1990) argues that the claim for "efficiency" as a policy goal is based on ideology, not science. He uses the word "ideology" not in a pejorative sense but rather in the sense of "a shared system of meaning and comprehension." Efficiency is not an objective goal but rather an opinion based on the system of beliefs embodied in the worldview of the Walrasian system. Bromley points out that a (probably unintended) consequence of Arrow's theorem was to divert public policy from democratic deliberation to the market. The first sentence in Arrow's book *Social Choice and Individual Values* (1951) states: "In a capitalist democracy there are essentially two methods by which social choices can be made: voting typically used to make 'political' decisions, and the market mechanism, typically used to make 'economic' decisions" (quoted in Bromley 1990, 92). The competitive market, with all the built-in assumptions that term implies, was a reliable mechanism to "scientifically" allocate resources to their most efficient uses without resorting to the messy (and "inefficient") process of democratic debate (sometimes called "the decision-making approach"). But as we have seen above, the identification of efficiency improvements (PPIs) not only is based on dubious behavioral assumptions, but it is also plagued by internal inconsistencies in the Walrasian system.

SUMMARY

In spite of mounting empirical evidence and a large body of theory demonstrating the logical inconsistencies and empirical shortcomings of Walrasian welfare economics, this framework continues to dominate economic textbooks. However, leading theorists, including many recent Nobel Prize winners in economics, have all but abandoned that framework. Judging from the contents of the leading economics journals, day-to-day work by applied economists is curiously disconnected from current work in mainstream economic theory. A time lag between theoretical frontiers and everyday practice is normal in any science, but its consequences are severe in the case of economic valuation. Current U.S. policies on climate change and biodiversity preservation, for example, rely heavily on welfare economic models whose legitimacy depends crucially on questionable theoretical formulations and on assumptions known to be wildly at odds with actual human behavior. Particularly problematic is the use of the concept of a potential Pareto improvement (PPI) as one of the major economic tools for evaluating alternative economic policies.

In a way Arrow's impossibility theorem summarizes the paradoxes discussed above. There is no way to aggregate the preferences of self-regarding individuals. The fatal flaw in Walrasian theory is that it cannot handle interdependencies among economic actors. Feldman (1987, 894) summarizes the uncomfortable state of neoclassical welfare economics after Arrow's theorem:

> Where does welfare economics stand today? The First and Second Theorems are encouraging results that suggest the market mechanism has great virtue: competitive equilibrium and Pareto optimality are firmly bound. But measuring the size of the economic pie, or judging among divisions of it, leads to paradoxes and impossibilities summarized by the Third Theorem. And this is a tragedy. We feel we know, like Adam Smith knew, which policies would increase the wealth of nations. But because of all our theoretic goblins, we can no longer prove it.

Perhaps the most important lesson for the theoretical literature in welfare economics is that we cannot do welfare economics without making interpersonal comparisons of utility. Many of the paradoxes and impossibilities embedded in Walrasian welfare economics arise from the attempt to avoid interpersonal comparisons of utility. People are, in fact, other regarding, and we cannot accurately portray economic behavior without accepting this fact. This observation dovetails with empirical findings from game theory and behavioral economics. Preferences are socially constructed and behavior is other regarding. This is the subject of the next chapter.

APPENDIX

Arrow's Impossibility Theorem

A formal (short version) definition of the Third Fundamental Theorem of Welfare Economics from the *New Palgrave Dictionary of Economics* is: "There is no Arrow Social Welfare function that satisfies the conditions of universality, Pareto consistency, neutrality-independence-monotonicity, and non-dictatorship." Arrow's theorem is sometimes called the **paradox of voting** and it can be illustrated as follows. Suppose we have three individuals (A, B, and C) with the following preferences for states of the economy (x, y, and z).

Person	Rank		
	1st	2nd	3rd
A	x	y	z
B	y	z	x
C	z	x	y

Suppose we do the "voting" in two stages. First we choose between x and y, and x is preferred to y by 2:1. Next we choose between y and z, and y is preferred to z by 2:1. This gives us the ranking in order of preference: x, y, z. But suppose we begin by choosing between x and z. In this case z is preferred to x by 2:1. Then we choose between x and y, and x is preferred 2:1. This gives us a different ranking: y, z, x.

The Microfoundations of Macroeconomics

The rise of Walrasian economics as a description of consumer and firm behavior combined with the notion of general equilibrium led naturally to using the same barter framework to describe entire economies. The model we first saw in Chapter 1 of individuals sitting around a table directly trading CDs became the preferred way to examine activity in regions, nations, and even the world economy. The concerns of classical economics—the distribution of income among economic classes or the long-term availability of natural resources, for example—were forgotten altogether or shoehorned into the Walrasian constrained optimization model. The utility function we saw in Chapter

1 became an aggregate demand function and production was analyzed in terms of aggregate supply. The applicability of marginal analysis to the macroeconomy was largely unexamined. Consider the idea of the "marginal product of labor" for the U.S. economy. What does it mean to examine the effect of adding a unit of labor to the whole economy, keeping everything else unchanged?

We can see how the barter economy model operates at the macro level by examining the **quantity equation,** the starting point for monetary economics, a school of thought popularized by Milton Friedman in the 1970s and 1980s. The quantity equation is:

$$(6.1) \qquad MV \equiv PQ$$

The left side of the equation shows the amount of money spent in a year. M is the money supply and V is velocity, or the number of times a unit of money (a dollar or a Euro) is spent during a particular time period, usually one year. So MV is the total amount of money consumers spend on goods and services in a year. The right side of the equation, PQ shows the value of goods sold in year. P is price of goods and Q is the physical quantity of goods. The equation is an identity because, obviously, the monetary value of goods sold must equal the monetary value of goods bought.

Monetarists made some strong assumptions about the quantity equation based on Walrasian economics. First, they assumed that the **velocity of money** was constant, that is, the proportions of money consumers decide to spend or save does not change appreciably over time. Second, they assumed that the real economy (the physical production of goods and services) is unaffected by the money supply. This is the no-money-illusion assumption imported into macroeconomics. If these assumptions are true, then the only effect of a change in the money supply, M, is to change the price level, P. Two policy implications of the quantity equation, and these assumptions, are (1) monetary policy (changing the money supply) can have no effect on the real economic activity, and (2) inflation is caused only by increases in the money supply (too many dollars chasing too few goods).

The monetarists used the quantity equation to argue for a "hands-off" economic policy on the part of governments. The only role of the monetary authority should be to keep the money supply growing at the same (constant) rate as real output, Q—so there would be no inflationary tendency. **Monetarism** has fallen out of favor because, among other things, it has been shown that neither basic assumption of the quantity equation holds—V is not constant and the real economy, Q, is affected by changes in the money supply, M. But the quantity equation (and monetary theory) is a good example of how macroeconomic theory and policies arise directly from the model of a simple barter economy and the assumptions economists make to jump from there to a market economy with money and prices.

GLOSSARY

Boadway paradox—When comparing alternatives, the one with the highest net gain is not necessarily the "best" one as judged by the Kaldor–Hicks compensation test.

Cycling paradox—If a movement from one point to another in utility space can be shown to be Pareto improving according to the Kaldor–Hicks criterion, then it may also be shown that a movement back to the original point is also Pareto improving.

General equilibrium—Economic equilibrium in all interrelated markets in the economy.

Hicksian income—The amount of economic product that is left for consumption after all capital stocks have been maintained intact. Some economists refer to this as "wealth" or "wealth per capita." It is GNP adjusted for externalities and capital (including "natural capital") depreciation.

Homothetic utility functions—A homothetic utility function implies that along the expansion path of consumption, indifference curves will have the same slopes. The marginal rate of substitution between two goods does not change as income increases. The utility maximizing proportion of all goods consumed remains exactly the same as income increases.

Ideology of efficiency—A term coined by Daniel Bromley to describe the mindset of economists who believe that the scope of economics is to identify potential Pareto improvements.

Microfoundations—The application of Walrasian theories of the consumer and firm to the analysis of the macroeconomy.

Monetarism—A school of economic thought, led by the late Milton Friedman, that advocates minimal government involvement in economic life. Monetarists argue that neither fiscal nor monetary policy is effective in stabilizing the economy or encouraging economic growth.

Paradox of voting—Arrow's impossibility theorem.

Partial equilibrium—Part of the economy is in equilibrium without reference to the rest of the economy. All prices and quantities outside that partial market are assumed to be constant and unaffected by changes within the partial market.

Positive economics—The view that economics should be about "what is" rather than "what ought to be." This is the rationale for trying to avoid interpersonal comparisons of utility.

Quantity equation—An equation for the macroeconomy showing the identity of the amount of money spent by consumers and the amount money received by producers (sellers) of those goods and services. It is written as $MV \equiv PQ$ and is the basic equation of monetary economics.

Real economy—The physical production of goods and services without reference to prices or money.

Velocity of money—The number of times a unit of money (a dollar or a Euro) is spent during a particular time period, usually one year.

REFERENCES AND FURTHER READING

Overviews of Welfare Theory

Bowles, S., and H. Gintis. 2000. Walrasian economics in retrospect. *Quarterly Journal of Economics* 115, 1411–1439.

Chipman, J., and J. Moore. 1978. The new welfare economics 1939–1974. *International Economic Review* 19, 547–584.

Feldman, A. 1987. Welfare economics. In *The New Palgrave Dictionary of Economics*, vol. 4, ed. J. Eatwell, M. Milgate, and P. Newman. London and New York: Macmillan, 889–895.

Fisher, F. 1983. *Disequilibrium Foundations of Equilibrium Economics*. Cambridge: Cambridge University Press.

Lockwood, B. 1987. Pareto efficiency. In *The New Palgrave Dictionary of Economics*, vol. 3, ed. J. Eatwell, M. Milgate, and P. Newman. London and New York: Macmillan, 811–813.

Varian, H. 1992. *Microeconomic Analysis*, 3rd ed. New York: Norton.

Early Critiques of Welfare Theory

Gorman, W. M. 1955. The intransitivity of certain criteria used in welfare economics. *Oxford Economic Papers*, new series, 7, 25–35.

Samuelson, P. 1950. Evaluation of real national income. *Oxford Economic Papers*, new series, 2, 1–29.

Scitovsky, T. 1941. A note on welfare propositions in economics. *Review of Economic Studies* 9, 77–88.

More Recent Theoretical Critiques

Albert, M., and R. Hahnel. 1990. *A Quiet Revolution in Welfare Economics*. Princeton, NJ: Princeton University Press.

Bromley, D. 1990. The ideology of efficiency: Searching for a theory of policy analysis. *Journal of Environmental Economics and Management* 19, 86–107.

Gowdy, J. 2004. The revolution in welfare economics and its implications for environmental valuation. *Land Economics* 80, 239–257.

Koning, N., and R. Jongeneel. 1997. Neo-Paretian welfare economics: Misconceptions and abuses. Wageningen Economic Papers, 05-97, Wageningen University, The Netherlands.

Stiglitz, J., 1994. *Whither Socialism?* Cambridge, MA: MIT Press.

van den Bergh, J. C. M., and J. Gowdy. 2003. The microfoundations of macroeconomics: An evolutionary perspective. *Cambridge Journal of Economics* 27, 65–84.

Social Choice Theory and Cost-Benefit Analysis

Arrow, K. 1951. *Social Choice and Individual Values*. New Haven, CT: Yale University Press.

Boadway, R. 1974. The welfare foundations of cost-benefit analysis. *Economic Journal* 47, 926–939.

Brekke, Kjell. 1997. The numeraire matters in cost-benefit analysis. *Journal of Public Economics* 64, 117–123.

Bryant, W. 1994. Misinterpretations of the second fundamental theorem of welfare economics: Barriers to better economic education. *Journal of Economic Education*, Winter, 75–80.

Chipman, J. 1974. The welfare ranking of Pareto distributions. *Journal of Economic Theory* 9, 275–282.

Chipman, J., and J. Moore. 1976. Why an increase in GNP need not imply an improvement in potential welfare. *Kyklos* 29, 391–418.

Stavins, R., A. Wagner, and G. Wagner. 2002. Interpreting sustainability in economic terms: Dynamic efficiency plus intergenerational equity. Discussion paper 02-29, August. Washington, DC: Resources for the Future.

Suzumura, K. 1999. Paretian welfare judgements and Bergsonian social choice. *Economic Journal* 109, 204–221.

7

THE BEHAVIORAL CRITIQUE OF WALRASIAN WELFARE ECONOMICS

Utility cannot be divorced from emotion, and emotions are triggered
by changes. A theory of choice that completely ignores feelings such
as the pain of losses and the regret of mistakes is not only
descriptively unrealistic, it also leads to prescriptions that do not
maximize the utility of outcomes as they are actually experienced.
— *Daniel Kahneman, "Maps of Bounded Rationality: Psychology for
Behavioral Economics,"* American Economic Review 93(5) (2003), 1457

Formidable criticisms of the behavioral assumptions of economic theory have
been made for a century or more. Thorstein Veblen wrote this eloquent para-
graph about economic man in 1898.

The hedonistic conception of man is that of a lightning calculator of pleasures
and pain, who oscillates like a homogeneous globule of desire of happiness under the
impulse of stimuli that shift him about the area, but leave him intact. He has neither
antecedent nor consequence. He is an isolated, definite human datum in stable equilibrium except for the buffets of the impinging forces that displace him in one direction or another. Self-imposed in elemental space, he spins symmetrically about his
own spiritual axis until the parallelogram of forces bears down upon him, where-
upon he follows the line of the resultant. When the force of the impact is spent, he
comes to rest, a self-contained globule of desire as before. (Veblen 1898, 389–391)

Criticisms like Veblen's have had little effect on mainstream economics partly
because they can be dismissed as "unscientific." As long as the arguments about

This chapter was originally published in a somewhat different form in John M. Gowdy, "Behavioral
Economics and Climate Change Policy," *Journal of Behavioral Economics and Organization* 68 (2008),
632–644. Reprinted with permission from Elsevier Publishers, Amsterdam.

human behavior are based on "armchair theorizing" and not empirical evidence about actual human behavior, criticisms can easily be ignored. But in recent decades, behavioral research has fundamentally changed the field of economics by putting it on a firm experimental basis. In its early days, behavioral economics concentrated on revealing various shortcomings of the standard model of economic choice. Recently, the field has moved from merely reacting against the rational actor model to identifying behavioral regularities that might form the basis for a more realistic model of human decision making. Experiments such as the **Ultimatum Game** and the Public Goods Game have established a number of regularities in human behavior, such as **loss aversion, habituation,** pure altruism, **altruistic punishment,** and inconsistent discounting of the future. These behavioral patterns have been confirmed by neurological experiments showing how behavior is reflected in brain activity.

BEHAVIORAL ECONOMICS AND GAME THEORY

For many years game theory was one of the bastions of orthodoxy in economics. The classic textbook example of the inevitability of selfish behavior is the **Prisoner's Dilemma** (PD). The setting for the PD game is this. The police have captured two people—the Gecko brothers, Seth and Quentin—suspected of committing a serious crime. The case against them is not strong, so a confession is needed from at least one of them. The police put the two brothers in separate rooms and offer them the deal shown in Figure 7.1. If neither confesses they get three years of prison time each. If they both confess they get four years each. If one confesses and the other does not, the confessor gets one year and the non-confessor gets six years. The way the game is framed, it is "rational" for Seth and Quentin to confess no matter what the other one does. Suppose Seth confesses; then Quentin should confess in order to get four years instead of six. Suppose Seth does not confess; then Quentin should also confess in this case to get one year instead of three.

The same logic applies to Seth, who should also confess no matter what Quentin does. This is called a **Nash Equilibrium** (named for Nobel laureate John Nash), which occurs when each player's strategy is optimal, given the

Seth

	Confess	Do not confess
Quentin Confess	4 years each	1 year for Quentin 6 years for Seth
Do not confess	6 years for Quentin 1 year for Seth	3 years each

Figure 7.1. The Prisoner's Dilemma

strategies of the other players. A player has a **dominant strategy** if that player's best strategy does not depend on what other players do (as in the PD—always confess).

The theoretical result of the PD game, no cooperation, is based on the assumption that there is no interaction between the two players. But in repeated PD games, people tend to cooperate. More surprisingly, even in one-shot anonymous PD experiments, over one-half of the players cooperate (Field 2001). Among the first two people to play the game in the 1950s were the imminent economist and mathematician Armen Alchian and John Williams, a distinguished mathematician at the Rand Corporation. When they cooperated in the one-shot PD game John Nash remarked, "I would have thought them more rational" (quoted in Field 2001).

Another classic game theory experiment is the Ultimatum Game (UG), which has been one of the most important contributions to behavioral economics. Like the Prisoner's Dilemma game before it, the UG helped revolutionize the way economists think about economic decision making. In this game, a leader offers one of two participants a certain sum of money and instructs that participant to share it with the second player. The second

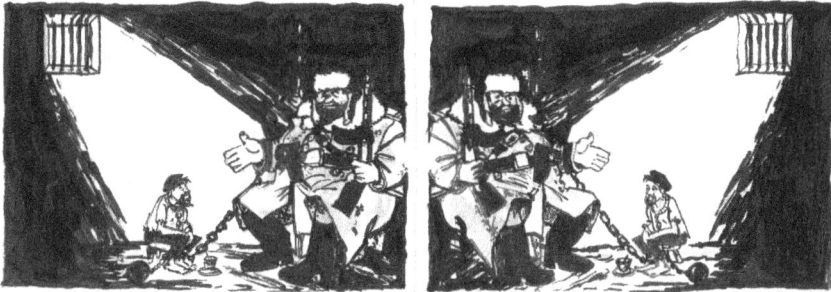

THE PRISONER'S DILEMMA

player can either accept the offer or reject it, in which case neither player gets anything. If the players behave according to the model of *Homo economicus*, the first player should offer the minimum amount and the second player should accept any positive offer. Results from the game show, however, that the majority of proposers in Western countries offer between 40 and 50 percent of the total and that offers under 30 percent of the total are usually rejected because they are not "fair" (Nowak, Page, and Sigmund 2000). These results have held up even when the game is played with substantial amounts of real money.

An extensive study using the UG game involved economists and anthropologists who played the game in fifteen different cultures around the world (Henrich et al. 2001, 73). The authors of the study concluded: "The canonical model of self-interested behavior is not supported in *any* society studied." As mentioned above, UG results are consistent in advanced market economies in North American, Europe and Japan. Among other cultures, such as the ones studied by Henrich and his colleagues, the results varied wildly depending on the social norms of the particular cultures studied. Among the whale-hunting Lamalera of Indonesia, 63 percent of the proposers divided the pie equally, and most of those who did not, offered more than 50 percent (the mean offer was 57 percent). In real life, a large catch, always the product of cooperation among many individual whalers, is meticulously divided into predesignated parts and carefully distributed among the members of the community. Among the Au and Gnau of the New Guinea Highlands, many proposers offered more than half the amount they had, and many of these "hyper-fair" offers were rejected! This reflects the Melanesian culture of status-seeking through gift giving. Making a large gift is a bid for social dominance in everyday life in these societies, and rejecting the gift is a rejection of being subordinate.

Another standard game is the Public Goods (PG) game. This game has many variants but a typical version goes something like this: There are ten players and they play the game for ten rounds. On each round each player is given the choice of depositing some amount of money (say 50¢) in "community pool" or keeping a larger amount for himself (say $1). For each player in turn, if the player deposits 50¢ in the common pool, then all the players get 50¢ each. So if all players are cooperative, then each player receives $5 per round ($10 \times 50$¢) for a total of $50 at the end of the ten-round game. If all players are selfish, they each only get $1 per round or $10 at the end of the game. The catch is that if one player acts selfishly and the other players cooperate, the selfish player gets $5.50 per round ($9 \times 50$¢ $+ $1) and all the others get $4.50 ($9 \times 50$¢). So it pays to be a defector (**free rider**) not a cooperator. Standard welfare theory predicts that "rational" players would never cooperate and that each player would take $1 for him- or herself starting with round one of the game. But results of PG games show much more complicated behavior. Typically, the majority of players begin by cooperating but then they change their behavior to defecting when they see others being selfish. If the game is played many times, people build up a sense of trust and there is a return to cooperation. If players are allowed to punish free riders by fining them, the game usually evolves to a cooperative outcome (for a summary of PG games see Gintis 2000, chapter 11, and Fehr and Gächter 2000a).

Results from the Ultimatum Game, the Public Goods game, and other game theoretic experiments show that, in a variety of settings and under a variety of assumptions, other-regarding motives are a better predictor of behavior than those embodied in self-regarding *Homo economicus*. Humans regularly exhibit a culturally conditioned sense of fairness, and they are willing to enforce cultural norms even at economic cost to themselves. Cross-cultural UG experiments also show that cultural norms vary greatly and that these norms dramatically affect the average amount offered in the game and the rates of rejection (Henrich et al. 2001). Again, a striking result of UG experiments is that the model of rational economic man is not supported in any culture studied (Henrich et al. 2001, 73). Henrich and his colleagues summarize their findings:

> Recent investigations have uncovered large, consistent deviations from the predictions of the textbook representation of *Homo economicus* (Alvin E. Roth et al., 1991; Ernst Fehr and Simon Gächter, 2000[b]; Colin Camerer, 2001). One problem appears to lie in economists' canonical assumption that individuals are entirely self-interested: in addition to their own material payoffs, many experimental subjects appear to care about fairness and reciprocity, are willing to change the distribution of material outcomes at personal cost, and are willing to reward those who act in a cooperative manner while punishing those who do not, even when these actions are costly to the individual. (Henrich et al. 2001, 73)

It took several decades of carefully designed, repeatable experiments to expose rational economic man as an inadequate model of human behavior. Economists and behavioral scientists are now turning their attention to the more difficult but potentially more important task of constructing an alternative to *Homo economicus* based on observed patterns of human behavior.

EMPIRICALLY ESTABLISHED BEHAVIORAL PATTERNS

Experimental results from behavioral economics, evolutionary game theory, and neuroscience have firmly established that human choice is a social, not self-regarding, phenomenon (see the essays in Camerer, Loewenstein, and Rabin 2004). Two broad principles have emerged from the literature: (1) human decision making cannot be accurately predicted without reference to social context, and (2) regular patterns of decision making, including responses to rewards and punishments, can be predicted both within particular cultures and across cultures. Recent research shows that preferences are endogenous, that is, they depend on the individual's personal history, interaction with others, and the social context of individual choice. Several consistent patterns of **endogenous preferences** have been observed.

Loss Aversion

A well-documented behavioral pattern is that people are more concerned about avoiding losses than they are about acquiring gains (Kahneman and Tversky 1991; Knetsch and Sinden 1984). The explicit assumption in economic analysis is that only the absolute magnitude of the change matters, not the direction of the change. Consumers routinely violate this assumption as advertisers know well. Most people would prefer to buy an item listed at $105 with a $5 discount than an item listed at $95 with a $5 surcharge, even though the price is the same in both cases ($100). Loss aversion is closely connected to the **endowment effect.**

The Endowment Effect

The hypothesis that losses are systematically valued more than equivalent gains has been verified in numerous experiments. It seems to be a psychological law that people prefer to keep something they already have compared with acquiring something they do not have (Kahneman and Tversky 1979). Tests of the endowment effect have shown that it is not due to wealth effects, income disparities, strategic behavior, or transactions costs (Kahneman, Knetsch, and Thaler 1991). Dozens of experiments show that preferences depend on the direction of the change, that is, whether people are paid to give up something they have or have to pay to get something they do not have (Knetsch 2007). The psychological model makes good predictions of economic behavior; the rational actor model does not.

Process-Regarding Preferences

People care about process as well as outcome. In designing economic policies, the process of arriving at a decision may be as important for public acceptance as the actual outcome itself. For example, results from the Ultimatum Game, (mean offers and rejection rates) vary significantly according to the process through which money is obtained and the way offers are made. Offers are substantially lower if proposers win their position by doing well on a quiz (Hoffman et al. 1994). Rejection rates are much lower if respondents are told that the offers were generated by a computer. In the Prisoner's Dilemma game, defection rates are significantly higher if the game is referred to as the "Wall Street Game" rather than the "Community Game." Results from these and numerous other studies in game theory, experimental economics, and behavioral economics show that models that do not take into account social processes such as community norms about fairness may lead to poor predictors of economic behavior.

Time Inconsistency and Hyperbolic Discounting

Time consistency is critical to the standard economic assumption that benefits delivered in the future should be discounted at a fixed rate. But behavioral studies indicate that people discount the near future at a higher rate than the distant future, and they have different discount rates for different kinds of outcomes (Frederick, Loewenstein, and O'Donoghue 2004). Anticipation has been found to be a positive thing in itself and may result in something in the future actually having a *higher* value. This finding is relevant to environmental policies such as preserving national parks and other wildlife areas because individuals may enjoy them more in the future (after retirement, for example) and the anticipation of this is important.

Biased Cultural Transmission

Biased cultural transmission is a theory of innovation diffusion based on the observation that people imitate others whose actions they trust or respect. People use heuristics, mental shortcuts, and rules of thumb to make otherwise complicated decisions. Biased cultural transmission may lead to the widespread adoption of economically inefficient ways of doing things. By *selectively* imitating respected individuals, people may ensure that innovations become established in a community whether or not the innovation is superior to others as determined by cost-benefit calculations (Henrich 2003). The important factor in adoption is the innovation's conformance with established cultural patterns. This has far-reaching implications for the design of economic policies.

Results from game theory and behavioral economics show that preferences are other regarding. People act to affect the well-being of others, positively or negatively, even at significant cost to themselves (Fehr and Gächter 2000a). A sense of fairness, including pure altruism, is a critical factor in economic decisions. This is illustrated in various game theory experiments such as the Public Goods game in which participants are willing to impose, at great cost to themselves, punishments on non-contributors, even in the last round of the game (Bowles and Gintis 2002). These kinds of behavior patterns have important consequences for judgments about human well-being and economic policy design.

THE EVOLUTIONARY BASIS OF HUMAN BEHAVIOR

Also relevant to the study of human decision making is a growing body of evidence from (nonhuman) animal experiments. These experiments show two important things. First, some social animals, such as primates, also have a sense of fairness and a tendency to cooperate. Second, some "lower" animals may behave closer to the rational actor model than humans do. They are self-regarding in evaluating payoffs, they are not susceptible to the **sunk-cost effect,** and they apparently evaluate payoffs according to expected utility theory. As discussed below, animal experiments show that human behavior has an evolutionary basis. They also illuminate the uniqueness of human behavior as occurring within a complex, socially constructed system. Ironically, it is not "rationality" that makes us human, but rather it is the "anomalies" uncovered by behavioral science.

The Behavior of Social Animals

Melis, Hare, and Tomasello (2006) played a cooperation game with chimpanzees at the Ngamba Island Chimpanzee Sanctuary in Uganda. A feeding platform with two metal rings was placed outside a testing room cage with a rope threaded through the rings and the two ends of the rope in the test room cage. If the chimpanzee(s) pulled only on one end of the rope, the rope passed through the rings and the food was not obtained. Only if two chimpanzees pulled together could the platform be pulled forward and the food obtained.

During repeated tests, the chimpanzees were allowed to recruit partners of their own choice, and they quickly learned to recruit those who were the best collaborators. Kin selection is not involved because the chimpanzees at the sanctuary are unrelated orphans from the wild. The authors observe: "Therefore, recognizing when collaboration is necessary and determining who is the best collaborative partner are skills shared by both chimpanzees and humans, so such skills may have been present in their common ancestor before humans evolved their own complex forms of collaboration" (Melis, Hare, and Tomasello 2006, 1297).

As we have seen, there is no place for interactive behavior, including altruism, in the basic Walrasian model. Economists also tend to be skeptical of altruistic behavior because of the free-rider problem. Free riders can out-compete altruists by taking advantage of their generosity. In the standard welfare model they will always out-compete altruists. As an answer to this objection, Henrich and his colleagues (2006, 1767) propose that altruism arose in humans hand in hand with punishing noncooperators. Altruistic punishment—punishing others for violating social norms even at cost to oneself—is one way humans deal with free riders and make cooperation work. Apparently, punishing those who do not cooperate actually stimulates the same pleasure centers in the brain that are activated by, for example, eating something sweet (Vogel 2004, 1131). Some evidence indicates that punishing behavior is present in chimpanzees. In one experiment, semi-wild chimpanzees were fed at a regular time only after all the chimpanzees in the compound came to the feeding station. Latecomers held up the feeding for all the chimps, and these stragglers were punished with hitting and biting.

A sense of what is fair and what is unfair is also present in our primate cousins. Brosnan and de Waal (2003) found that brown capuchin monkeys (*Cebus paella*) exhibit a strong aversion to inequity. In one experiment, monkeys rejected rewards for performing a simple task if they witnessed another monkey receiving a more desirable reward for performing the same task. Pairs of monkeys were trained to exchange a small rock with a human experimenter in return for a piece of cucumber. When one monkey saw the other receiving a more desirable reward (a grape), the first monkey would not only refuse to participate in further exchanges but would frequently refuse to eat the cucumber reward, sometimes even throwing it toward the human experimenter. Brosnon and de Wall (2003, 299) write: "People judge fairness based both on the distribution of gains and on the possible alternatives to a given outcome. Capuchin monkeys, too, seem to measure reward in relative terms, comparing their own rewards with those available, and their own efforts with those of others."

In terms of standard economic theory, the question is not whether humans (or other animals) are selfish or altruistic but whether they are *other regarding*. As shown in Chapter 1, if individuals evaluate their payoffs based on what others get, this violates the conditions for Pareto efficiency in the standard model. Other-regarding behavior may be altruistic, envious, or any other socially conditioned response to others. For example, researchers found that in cooperation games with an opportunity to punish, subjects from Belarus and Russia punished not only defectors but also strong cooperators (Vogel 2004)!

Are "Lower" Animals More Rational than Humans?

The view of the human rational actor as a highly evolved decision maker has also taken a blow from studies of animals with more limited cognitive ability. Regarding the claims for human rationality, it is ironic that a large body of evidence suggests that some lower animals act more in accordance with the economic model of rational choice than humans do. In a classic experiment, Harper (1982) tested the ability of a flock of ducks to achieve a stable Nash Equilibrium when fed balls of bread. Every morning two researchers would stand on the bank of the pond where the ducks were and throw out five-gram dough balls at different intervals. Expected utility theory would predict that the ducks would distribute themselves between the two feeders in such a way that $N1/r1 = N2/r2$, where Ni is the number of ducks and ri is the expected (bread) payoff from standing in front of one of the feeders. So if there are thirty-three ducks participating and if one experimenter throws a five-gram ball of dough every fifteen seconds and the other experimenter throws a five-gram ball of dough every thirty seconds, there should be twenty-two ducks in front of the first experimenter and eleven in front of the other. And in fact this is what happened. The ducks rearranged their numbers efficiently as the payoffs were changed. Furthermore, when the experimenters changed the speed of throwing the dough balls, the ducks would quickly and efficiently readjust their numbers. Glimcher (2002, 329) writes:

> One thing that was particularly striking about this result was the speed at which the ducks achieved this assortment. After 90 seconds of breadball throwing, as few as ten breadballs have been dispersed. Long before half the ducks have obtained even a single breadball, they have produced a precise equilibrium solution.

A well-known violation of rationality is the sunk-cost effect. Ignoring unrecoverable past expenditures is one the common admonishments for students learning to "think like an economist," that is to behave in a sophisticated rational way (Frank and Bernanke 2004). But once again, actual human behavior consistently deviates from the rational actor ideal. A number of experiments have demonstrated that human decisions are strongly influenced by sunk costs. It appears, however, that ignoring sunk costs is a characteristic of the behavior of lower animals but not of humans (Arkes and Ayton 1999). Fantino (2004) performed a simple investment experiment with college students and pigeons. Both were rewarded with money or food for pressing a computer keyboard an undetermined number of times until an award was given. Pressing some of the keys resulted in an award whereas pressing others produced no reward. The experiment was designed to model a bad investment in which the chances of success diminished as the number of responses increased. The more times a key was pressed with no reward forthcoming, the less likely further pressing would produce an award. In the experiment, the pigeons quickly switched from one key to another if an award failed to appear, whereas the students kept repeatedly pressing the same key—indicating that pigeons were less susceptible than students to the sunk-cost effect. In another sunk-cost experiment, Maestripieri and Alleva (1991) tested the behavior of mother mice in defending their young, and they found that the aggressiveness of their defensive behavior depended on the number of offspring in the litter rather than the amount of time invested in caring for them.

The animal behavior literature, together with observations of human behavior, suggests that letting sunk costs influence decision making is a trait that must have something to do with uniquely human characteristics such as the presence of complex capital investments and complex institutions in human societies. It is sometimes argued that although individuals may exhibit irrational behavior, such behavior can be corrected in groups (as in the rational expectations literature). In fact, research shows that groups are probably more susceptible to the sunk-cost effect than are individuals (Whyte 1993).

NEUROSCIENCE CONFIRMATION OF BEHAVIORAL REGULARITIES

A rapidly growing field is **neuroeconomics**, that is, identifying regularities in brain activity corresponding to specific human economic decisions. These neurological findings may not add anything new to the catalog of behavioral patterns observed by behavioral economics, but they do show that they are more than anomalies. These observed behaviors are not random mistakes but rather are a part of the neurological organization of the human brain.

Habituation

It has long been known that two groups of neurons, in the *ventral tegmental* and the *substantia nigra pars compacta* areas, and the dopamine they release are critical for reinforcing certain kinds of behavior (Glimcher, Dorris, and Bayer 2005; Schultz 2002). Schultz (2002) measured the activity of these neurons while thirsty monkeys sat quietly and listened for a tone that was followed by a squirt of fruit juice into their mouths. After a period of a fixed, steady amount of juice, the amount of juice was doubled without warning. The rate of neuron firing went from about three per second to eighty per second. As this new magnitude of reward was repeated, the firing rate returned to the baseline rate of three firings per second. The opposite happened when the reward was reduced without warning. The firing rate dropped dramatically but then returned to the baseline rate of three firings per second.

The Framing Effect

Consistency in choice is the hallmark of rational economic man, and it implies that the evaluation of choices is unaffected by the manner in which the choices are framed. This view was challenged by Kahneman and Tversky (1979) in their formulation of "prospect theory," that is, people evaluate changes in terms of a reference point. The "framing effect" means that the frame of reference may change according to how a particular choice is presented, and this will affect the payoff decision. This effect has been confirmed in numerous experiments, and it too seems to have a neurological basis. De Martino and his colleagues (2006) used functional magnetic resonance imaging (fMRI) to look at the neurological effects of framing in a simple experiment. A group of twenty British subjects were asked to choose between identical outcomes framed differently. They were told that they would initially receive £50. They then had to choose between a "sure" option and a "gamble" option. The sure option was presented in two ways, either as a gain (say, keep £20 of the £50) or as a loss (say, lose £30 of the £50). The gamble option was presented in the same way in both cases—a pie chart showing the probability of winning or losing. People responded differently depending on how the question was framed, and this was reflected in fMRI images. Different parts of the brain lit up depending on how the question was framed.

The fact that the framing effect found in this experiment had a neurological basis was confirmed: "Our data provide a neurobiological account of the framing effect, both within and across individuals. Increased activation in the amygdale was associated with subjects' tendency to be risk-averse in the Gain frame and risk-seeking in the Loss frame, supporting the hypothesis that the framing effect is driven by an affect heuristic underwritten by an emotional system" (De Martino et al. 2006, 686).

The neural basis for loss aversion was also confirmed by Tom and colleagues (2007). They found that in order for people to accept a fifty-fifty gamble the potential gain needs to be twice as high as the potential loss. They discovered that the brain regions that evaluated potential gains and losses were more sensitive to losses. Also, between-subject differences in loss aversion reflected between-subject differences in neural responses.

Threshold Effects

In a study of how rhesus monkeys respond in a color matching experiment, Schall and Thompson (1999) found a correlation between neural firing rates and making a physical movement. Thirsty monkeys were trained to stare at a cross in the center of a blank display. Then a circle of eight spots were illuminated, seven in one color and the eighth in another. If the monkey moved his gaze to look at the "oddball" color he was rewarded with a squirt of juice. When the oddball color was identified, neural firing rates began to increase at the location in the brain encoding the oddball. Only after the neural firing rate passes an apparently fixed threshold did the monkey move his gaze. Glimcher, Dorris, and Bayer (2005) postulate that the decision-making brain forms a kind of topological map that encodes something such as the relative expected gains of each possible choice. Actually making a choice (taking an action) depends on the strength of the signal relating to that particular action (the neural firing threshold).

The finding that some animals behave according to the rational actor model can be interpreted in very different ways. The view is widespread that animal behavior justifies the economic rational actor model. Gintis (2007, 7), for example, argues that the assumption of choice consistency among humans is justified by animal behavior: "Economic and biological theory thus have a natural affinity; the choice consistency on which the rational actor model of economic theory depends is rendered plausible by biological evolutionary theory, and the optimization techniques pioneered by economic theorists are routinely applied and extended by biologists in modeling the behavior of a vast array of organisms." Others take the view that animal studies show that the rational choice model is inappropriate to describe all but the simplest kinds of human decision making. Camerer, Loewenstein, and Prelec (2005, 55) write:

> Our view is that establishing a neural basis for some rational choice principles will not necessarily vindicate the approach as widely applied to *humans*. . . . Ironically, rational choice models might therefore be most useful in thinking about the simplest kinds of decisions humans and other species make—involving perceptual tradeoffs, motor movements, foraging for food and so forth—and prove least useful in thinking about abstract, complex, long-term tradeoffs which are the traditional province of economic theory.

Far from describing higher-order, complex human behavior, the axiomatic rational choice model strips away everything that makes humans unique as highly intelligent social animals. Nelson (2005, 264) puts it succinctly:

> Defining economics as the study of *rational choice*, neoclassical economics treats human physical bodies, their needs, and their evolved actual psychology of thought and action as rather irrelevant. The notion that humans are created as rational decision-makers is, from a physical anthropology point of view, just as ludicrous as the notion that humans were created on the sixth day.

Our very complex, other-regarding, altruistic, empathetic behavior is what makes humans unique, and understanding this behavior is the key to formulating effective economic policies having complicated and long-lasting consequences.

WHY DOES ALL THIS MATTER? THE IMPORTANCE OF BEHAVIORAL ASSUMPTIONS

At the core of neoclassical welfare theory is the rational actor model of human behavior. Individuals act to maximize utility according to consistent, constant, well-ordered, and well-behaved preferences. In the rational actor model, preferences are **exogenous**, that is, other individuals or social institutions do not influence them. The argument for using individual preferences as the starting point is a powerful one. It is a good thing for individuals to have what they want, and each individual is the best judge of what he or she wants. According to Randall (1988, 217), economists are "doggedly nonjudgmental about people's preferences." But are they? In fact, by forcing individual preferences through the narrow funnel of rational choice theory, economists are denying individuals a whole range of choices falling under the rubric of endogenous preferences.

For example, in surveys of consumer preferences for environmental services, information is collected that routinely violates the axioms of consumer choice theory. People express ethical concerns based on group norms (Fehr and Gächter 2000a; Gowdy and Seidel 2004), and considerable evidence exists that people value the medium and distant futures about the same (hyperbolic discounting) (Laibson 1997). But collected information about consumer

Expressed preferences		Eliminated by assuming		Policy implications
Lexicographic preferences	→	Continuity	→	Everything is tradable
Inconsistent discounting	→	Time consistency	→	Straight-line discounting
Endowment effect	→	Symmetric rationality	→	WTA = WTP
Other-regarding preferences	→	Independent choices	→	Relative income does not matter
Process-regarding preferences	→	Outcome-regarding preferences	→	Process does not matter

Figure 7.2. Preference filtering in the Walrasian model

attitudes is filtered by economists through the axioms of consumer choice to fit the stylized "facts" of neoclassical welfare economics (as shown in Figure 7.2). Thus subjectivism and values enter economics in a non-explicit way that is more dangerous than making explicit value judgments.

These filters take a variety of forms. For example, in surveys using the **contingent valuation method** (CVM), "protest bids" are very common. These may be in the form of extreme bids of zero or infinity. One reason for these bids is the existence of **lexicographic preferences,** that is, people may place absolute values on environmental preservation and refuse to make trade-offs between environmental features and money. Spash and Hanley (1995) found that approximately 25 percent of respondents in CVM surveys refused to consider the concept of trading income changes with changes in environmental quality. In many CVM surveys, these bids are excluded from the analysis thereby disenfranchising those respondents. A common finding is the existence of lexicographic preferences. In this case people have an absolute preference for something and are unwilling to except any substitute for that particular thing. A recent trend in CVM studies is to filter out lexicographic preferences by designing surveys to elicit market-compatible responses. Bid cards, for example, restrict choices in CVM surveys to a given set of offers, thus forcing them to conform to the normative assumptions of the investigator. Willingness to pay measures of the value of environmental goods are routinely used even though a considerable amount of evidence shows the correct measure to use is the willingness to avoid losses.

The theoretical and empirical breakthroughs described in this chapter and in Chapter 6 are beginning to significantly influence the theory and methods of economics. However, although economists rightly point out that mainstream theorists have extended the neoclassical paradigm far beyond the limits of traditional welfare analysis, the leading textbooks, and the policy recommendations of most economists, continue to rely almost exclusively on the basic framework of the Walrasian system. The prospects for a reorientation of economic theory and policy are discussed in the next two chapters.

GLOSSARY

Altruistic punishment—The willingness of economic actors to punish others who violate perceived social norms, even at substantial cost to themselves.

Biased cultural transmission—A theory of innovation diffusion based on the observation that people imitate others whose actions they trust or respect.

Contingent valuation method (CVM)—Soliciting consumer preferences using sophisticated questionnaires and interviewing techniques. The design and interpretation of CVM surveys are based on the standard economic model of rationality and consistency in choices.

Dominant strategy—A player's best strategy that does not depend on what the other players do.

Endogenous preferences—Preferences that depend upon (are endogenous to) social norms.

Endowment effect—People prefer to keep something they already have compared with acquiring something they do not have.

Exogenous preferences—Preferences that are independent of (exogenous to) social norms.

Framing effect—Changing the frame of reference may change the evaluation of choices.

Free rider—A selfish individual who takes advantage of the generosity of others. Given the behavioral assumptions of the standard model, free riders will always drive out altruists in a competitive situation.

Habituation—The perceived positive or negative benefits of gains or losses, if repeated, tend to disappear over time.

Hyperbolic discounting—People tend to discount the future more heavily in the immediate future than they do in the distant future.

Lexicographic preferences—These occur when a consumer infinitely prefers one good to another. In this case a commodity bundle containing more of the lexicographic good will be preferred to any other commodity bundle. Substitutability does not exist.

Loss aversion—People are willing to pay more to avoid the loss of something than they are willing to pay to gain something they do not have.

Nash Equilibrium—Occurs when each player's strategy is optimal, given the strategy of the other players.

Neuroeconomics—Testing the effects of economic decision making on brain activity using fMRI imaging or other measures of neurological activity.

Prisoner's Dilemma—The classic game theory experiment purportedly showing the inevitability of noncooperative behavior when players cannot interact.

Process-regarding preferences—People care about the process through which an outcome is obtained as well as the outcome itself.

Sunk-cost effect—Letting unrecoverable past expenditures influence the decision-making process. This is "irrational" in standard theory.

Threshold effect—In neuroscience experiments, actually making a choice (taking an action) depends on the strength of the signal relating to that particular action (the neural firing threshold). No action is taken until a certain threshold is reached.

Time inconsistency—People do not discount the future in a consistent way. People use different discount rates for different ranges of time.

Ultimatum Game—One of the first modern game theory experiments showing the pervasiveness of other-regarding behavior (altruistic punishment).

REFERENCES AND FURTHER READING

Altruism and Altruistic Punishment

Field, A. 2001. *Altruistically Inclined? The Behavioral Sciences, Evolutionary Theory, and the Origins of Reciprocity.* Ann Arbor: University of Michigan Press.

Henrich, J., R. McElreath, A. Barr, J. Ensminger, C. Barrett, A. Bolyanatz, J. Cardenas, M. Gurven, E. Gwako, N. Henrich, C. Lesorogol, F. Marlowe, D. Tracer, and J. Ziker. 2006. Costly punishment across human societies. *Science* 312, 1767–1770.

Vogel, G. 2004. The evolution of the golden rule. *Science* 303, 1128–1131.

Animal Behavior and Evolutionary Psychology

Arkes, H., and P. Ayton. 1999. The sunk cost and concorde effects: Are humans less rational than lower animals? *Psychological Bulletin* 125, 591–600.

Brosnan, S., and F. de Wall. 2003. Monkeys reject unequal pay. *Nature* 425, 297–299.

Harper, D. 1982. Competitive foraging in mallards: "Ideal free" ducks. *Animal Behavior* 30, 575–584.

Maestripieri, D., and E. Alleva. 1991. Litter defense and parental investment allocation in house mice. *Behavioral Processes* 56, 223–230.

Melis, A., B. Hare, and M. Tomasello. 2006. Chimpanzees recruit the best collaborators. *Science* 311, 1297–1300.

Behavioral Economics, Theory, and Policy

Bowles, S., and H. Gintis. 2002. Social capital and community governance. *Economic Journal* 112, F419–F436.

Camerer, C., G. Loewenstein, and M. Rabin (eds.). 2004. *Advances in Behavioral Economics.* Princeton, NJ: Princeton University Press.

Fantino, E. 2004. Behavior-analytic approaches to decision making. *Behavioral Processes* 66, 279–288.

Gowdy, J., and I. Seidl. 2004. Economic man and selfish genes: The relevance of group selection to economic policy. *Journal of Socio-Economics* 33, 343–358.

Henrich, J. 2003. Cultural group selection, coevolutionary processes and large-scale cooperation. *Journal of Economic Behavior and Organization* 53, 3–35.

Kahneman, D. 2003. Maps of bounded rationality: Psychology for behavioral economics. *American Economic Review* 93(5), 1449–1475.

Knetsch, J. 2007. Biased valuations, damage assessments, and policy choices: The choice of measure matters. *Ecological Economics* 63, 684–689.

Discounting and Time Preference

Frederick, S., G. Loewenstein, and T. O'Donoghue. 2004. Time discounting and time preference: A critical review. In C. Camerer, G. Lowenstein, and M. Rabin (eds.), *Advances in Behavioral Economics*. Princeton, NJ: Princeton University Press, 162–222.

Laibson, D., 1997. Golden eggs and hyperbolic discounting. *Quarterly Journal of Economics* 112, 443–477.

Games

Fehr, E., and S. Gächter. 2000a. Cooperation and punishment in public goods experiments. *American Economic Review* 90, 980–994.

Fehr, E., and S. Gächter. 2000b. Fairness and retaliation: The economics of reciprocity. *Journal of Economic Perspectives* 14(3), 159–181.

Gintis, H. 2000. *Game Theory Evolving*. Princeton, NJ: Princeton University Press.

Henrich, J., R. Boyd, S. Bowles, C. Camerer, E. Fehr, H. Gintis, and R. McElreath. 2001. In search of Homo economicus: Behavioral experiments in 15 small-scale societies. *American Economic Review* 91, 73–78.

Hoffman, E., K. McCabe, K. Shachat, and V. Smith. 1994. Preferences, property rights, and anonymity in bargaining games. *Games and Economic Behavior* 7, 346–380.

Nowak, M., K. Page, and K. Sigmund. 2000. Fairness versus reason in the ultimatum game. *Science* 289, 1773–1775.

Roth, A., V. Prasnikar, M. Okuno-Fujiwara, and S. Zamir. 1991. Bargaining and market behavior in Jerusalem, Ljubljana, Pittsburgh and Tokyo: An experimental study. *American Economic Review* 81(5), 1068–1095.

Neuroeconomics and Neuroscience

Camerer, C., G. Loewenstein, and D. Prelec. 2005. Neuroeconomics: How neuroscience can inform economics. *Journal of Economic Literature* 43, 9–64.

De Martino, B., D. Kumaran, B. Seymour, and R. Dolan. 2006. Frames, biases, and rational decision-making in the human brain. *Science* 313, 684–687.

Glimcher, P. 2002. Decisions, decisions, decisions: Choosing a biological science of choice. *Neuron* 36, 323–332.

Glimcher, P., M. Dorris, and H. Bayer. 2005. Physiological utility theory and the neuroeconomics of choice. *Games and Economic Behavior* 52, 213–256.

Schall, J., and K. Thompson. 1999. Neural selection and control of visually guided eye movements. *Annual Review of Neuroscience* 22, 241–259.

Schultz, W. 2002. Getting formal with dopamine and reward. *Neuron* 36, 241–263.

Tom, S., C. Fox, C. Trepel, and R. Poldrack. 2007. The neural basis of loss aversion in decision-making under risk. *Science* 315, 515–518.

Other References Cited

Camerer, C. 2001. *Behavioral Economics*. Princeton, NJ: Princeton University Press.

Frank, R., and B. Bernanke. 2004. *Principles of Economics*, 2nd ed. New York: McGraw-Hill.

Gintis, H. 2007. A framework for the integration of the behavioral sciences. *Behavioral and Brain Sciences* 30, 1–16.

Kahneman, D., J. Knetsch, and R. Thaler. 1991. The endowment effect, loss aversion, and status quo bias. *Journal of Economic Perspectives* 5, 193–206.

Kahneman, D., and A. Tversky. 1979. Prospect theory: An analysis of decision under risk. *Econometrica* 47, 263–291.

Kahneman, D., and A. Tversky. 1991. Loss aversion in riskless choices: A reference dependent model. *Quarterly Journal of Economics* 106, 1039–1061.

Knetsch, J., and J. Sinden. 1984. Willingness to pay and compensation demanded: Experimental evidence of an unexpected disparity in measures of value. *Quarterly Journal of Economics* 99, 507–521.

Nelson, J. 2005. Is economics a natural science? *Cosmos and History: The Journal of Natural and Social Philosophy* 2, 261–269.

Randall, A. 1988. What mainstream economists have to say about the value of biodiversity. In E. O. Wilson (ed.), *Biodiversity*. Washington, DC: National Academy Press, 217–223.

Spash, C., and N. Hanley. 1995. Preferences, information, and biodiversity preservation. *Ecological Economics* 12, 191–208.

Veblen, T. 1898. Why is economics not an evolutionary science? *Quarterly Journal of Economics* 12, 373–397.

Whyte, G. 1993. Escalating commitment in individual and group decision making: A prospect theory approach. *Organizational Behavior and Human Decision Processes* 54, 430–455.

8

COST-BENEFIT ANALYSIS
OLD AND NEW

Benefit-cost practice and policy analyses were greatly improved
when non-market, or non-pecuniary, values were included—a
change of relatively recent vintage, and still not universal. The
evidence now suggests further improvements could be made by
taking account of more realistic behavioral assumptions in valuing
gains and losses.
> —*Jack Knetsch, "Gains, Losses, and the US-EPA* Economic Analyses
> Guidelines: *A Hazardous Product,"* Environmental & Resource Economics
> *32 (2005), 110*

THE WELFARE FOUNDATIONS OF COST-BENEFIT ANALYSIS

The economic theory behind standard cost-benefit analysis (CBA) begins with
the basic assumptions about human preferences discussed in Part One of this
book. Economic value arises solely from human preferences and these preferences are stable over time (Stigler and Becker 1977). It is the task of econometricians to uncover these hidden but stable preferences through surveys
(such as the **contingent valuation** method) or by imputing prices for goods
not directly traded in markets (**hedonic pricing**). The object is to identify
potential Pareto improvements so that public policies can be designed to correct these inefficiencies (market failures). Whether or not market choices, or
pseudo-market choices, identified by CBA accurately reflect what is "best" for
society depends critically on the validity of the assumptions of the rational
actor model.

This chapter was originally published in a somewhat different form in John M. Gowdy, "Toward an
Experimental Foundation for Benefit-Cost Analysis," *Ecological Economics* 63 (2007), 649–655.
Reprinted with permission from Elsevier Publishers, Amsterdam.

My teacher Nicholas Georgescu-Roegen compared this process to Michelangelo's view that his statutes were already inside the marble blocks he began with—it was his job merely to uncover them. Likewise, in the minds of many econometricians, if there is some disparity between observed behavior and the *Homo economicus* ideal (for example, unstable preferences, other-regarding behavior, time inconsistency) it must be because we are using the wrong tools to uncover the "real" preferences we know are out there.

CBA estimates changes in economic welfare using the Marshallian concept of consumer surplus as discussed in the appendix to Chapter 5. These are market-based values that include both income and substitution effects. As we saw, changes in real income can cause distortions in estimated gains and losses. Recall the discussion in Chapter 5 of the three measures of welfare changes: consumer surplus, equivalent variation, and compensating variation. The theoretical justification for using consumer surplus in CBA is that, based on equation (5.1) ($E_{11} = E_{11 \text{ (utility held constant)}} - \alpha_1 E_{1M}$), if the budget share of the good (α_1) and/or its income elasticity (E_{1M}) is small, then there should be little or no difference between consumer surplus (measured by market prices) and the two income-adjusted (Hicksian) welfare measures. CBA advocates argue that for most goods this is likely to be the case (the classic paper making this point is Willig 1976).

A telling empirical criticism of the equivalence-of-welfare-measures argument is that observed differences between the various welfare measures are enormous. In contrast to the standard argument as to the unimportance of differences between compensating (willingness to pay for a gain, or WTP) and equivalent variations (willingness to accept a loss, or WTA), the evidence suggests that people evaluate the loss of a good or service (WTA) much higher than they do the gain of that same good or service (WTP). Ratios of WTA/WTP in actual studies, some using real money, range from 1.4 to 61.0 (Brown and Gregory 1999). A likely explanation of this discrepancy is the behavioral regularities, including **loss aversion** and the endowment effect, discussed in the last chapter.

Nevertheless, if we can use the consumer surplus measure, and we assume that well-being can be equated with (properly adjusted) measures of income, then the goal of CBA is to identify changes in resource allocation that increase total income, even if some people are made worse off. Most policy recommendations based on CBA focus on correcting relatively small (marginal) market imperfections.

Assumptions Embedded in Walrasian Cost-Benefit Analysis

1. Individuals are rational and consistent in their choices, and these choices can be revealed by economic analysis.

2. The socially best (more efficient) outcome is the sum of all the individual choices.

3. Market outcomes are reasonable indicators of the best (most efficient) use of scarce resources and represent a reasonably fair distribution of economic output.

4. When economic analysis reveals preferences different from market outcomes, this is an indication of market failure.

5. According to the Second Fundamental Theorem, market failures can be corrected by appropriate public policies.

The *theoretical* arguments against standard CBA are those discussed in Chapter 6 pointing out the inconsistencies in identifying potential Pareto improvements—the cycling problem, the Boadway paradox, and in general, the impossibility of drawing general equilibrium conclusions from partial equilibrium statements. The *behavioral* arguments against conventional CBA are discussed in the next section.

Cost-benefit analysis is one of the cornerstones of modern policy analysis. Over the years one of the major contributions of economics to public policy has been to use CBA to apply basic concepts such as opportunity cost, efficiency, and consumer sovereignty to decisions involving the expenditure of public funds. An examination of CBA shows both the power of economic reasoning and the limitations imposed on that reasoning by the assumptions of Walrasian welfare theory. In recent years, due both to the revolution in economic theory and to growing public distrust of CBA, the technique has come under increasing scrutiny (Ackerman and Heinzerling 2004; Revesz and

Livermore 2008). Applications of CBA have been most successful in cases involving specific, relatively small-scale projects. Current controversies surrounding CBA have arisen for the most part from its extension to include public policy decisions involving much longer time frames and much larger geographic scope.

THE BEHAVIORAL CRITIQUE OF TRADITIONAL CBA

As we saw in chapters 6 and 7, advances in economic theory and a growing body of behavioral findings call into question many of the underlying assumptions of the standard approach to economic valuation. The major points of departure between the assumptions of conventional CBA and the findings of contemporary behavioral economics are these:

Increasing Income May or May Not Increase Well-Being

Conventional CBA assumes that income is a reasonable measure of welfare (utility or well-being). The finding that income is not a good proxy for happiness has long been a topic of interest to economists, inspired by the pioneering work of Easterlin (1974) and others. Measures of **subjective well-being** show consistently that, past a certain fairly low level, increasing income does not lead to permanent increases in well-being. Real per capita income in the United States has increased sharply in recent decades but reported happiness has slightly declined. Studies of individuals also show a lack of correlation between increases in income and increases in happiness (Frey and Stutzer 2002). Past a certain income level, only relative income contributes to well-being, and beyond that level, as incomes go up everyone is on a zero-sum treadmill.

Recent work on the economics of well-being uses a direct measure of subjective utility as an alternative to per capita gross domestic product (GDP). Current work in quality of life indicators has resulted in theoretically sound measures of subjective well-being and suggests a much more robust approach to economic accounting for public policy than merely modifying existing income-based measures of social welfare. A number of economists advocate using measures of subjective well-being as an indicator of social welfare, and the object of public policy, rather than per capita GDP (Layard 2005). The implication of the well-being literature for CBA is that estimated increases in income resulting from a public project may not indicate an increase in well-being. Monetary estimates of market-based costs and benefits capture only a part of the picture (Spash 2007).

Loss Aversion

The finding that people are loss averse—people place a higher value on losing something they have than they do on gaining something they do not have—is well established (Knetsch 2005). Yet conventional CBA assumes that values are determined independently of a reference state. This is especially problematic when it comes to placing values on environmental features. Because most environmental valuation policy problems involve losses, this approach leads to a systematic bias toward undervaluing environmental features. Estimating the value of environmental quality to future generations almost always involves losses (loss of climate stability, nonrenewable resources, clean air and water). Loss aversion implies that if environmental protection polices are to respect human preferences then these polices should err on the side of caution. The **precautionary principle** was originally based on considerations of uncertainly and irreversibility. It is also justified by evidence from experimental economics.

The Psychology of Discounting

Discounting the future makes perfect sense for relatively short-term individual decisions involving money. For several reasons, including impatience, opportunity cost, and risk, for an individual making a decision today, receiving $100 today is better than receiving $100 a year from now. Discounting is also appropriate, for example, in the case of a local government deciding whether or not to build a new community center or to spend the money on highway improvements. But as we extend our time frame of reference, and as we broaden our policy considerations, discounting is more and more problematic. In the case of global climate change, catastrophic consequences occurring a hundred years or more in the future are inconsequential in terms of their present discounted value. In this case, as in the case of many other kinds of environmental damages, uncertainties multiply as we go farther into the future (Weitzman 2007b).

For long-term decisions involving risk and uncertainty, the way discounting is applied in traditional CBA is at odds with experimental results showing how people actually discount the future. Traditional CBA uses a single straight-line discount rate for everything from local development projects to evaluating far-in-the-distant-future effects of global climate change. Behavioral experiments have revealed that people use different discount rates for different circumstances. For example, under many circumstances, people discount the near future at a higher rate than the distant future (Laibson 1997). People also use different discount rates for different kinds of things (Gintis 2000). Money in a bank account is discounted differently than a scenic view, a happy life, or the future well-being of the human species. Anticipation may be a positive thing in itself so that something in the future may have a higher value than at the present. For example, preserving national parks and other wildlife areas is important because people anticipate using them in the future (after retirement, for example). Applying standard discount rates yields inappropriate estimates of future value in these cases (Weitzman 1998).

The Value of Gains and Losses Depend upon Social Context
In standard CBA, individual preferences are independent and additive. Social benefits and costs are typically calculated as the sum of the benefits and costs to individuals. These estimates assume that people care only about absolute income and not their income relative to others. By contrast, as discussed in the last chapter, experimental results show that economic behavior is based on preferences that are dependent upon social context and the relationship of individuals to others. This has been demonstrated in behavioral, game theoretic, and neurological experiments (Gintis 2000). Other-regarding behavior includes reciprocity, inequality aversion, pure altruism, spiteful or envious preferences, and altruistic punishment. Such preferences affect basic economic behavior. The implication for CBA of the relative income effect is that the benefits of a policy that raises the incomes of everyone might be overestimated in standard theory.

The Incommensurability Problem
Incommensurability refers to things that do not share a common standard of measure. As we saw in Part One, Walrasian theory assumes that there is some common denominator (utility) against which all things can be compared. When the theory is extended to market exchange, price is assumed to be the common denominator and an indicator of utility. Putting a price

on everything that gives well-being (value) to a person implicitly makes everything substitutable. Behavioral research and economic surveys have shown that lexicographic preferences are widespread—there are many things that people are not willing to part with regardless of the price offered for them. This is a particularly important issue in the case of environmental features.

Purely monetary measures of costs and benefits tend to overestimate the costs of implementing regulatory policies and underestimate the value of the benefits of those policies. Ackerman and Heinzerling (2004) looked at three examples of regulatory success—the removal of lead from gasoline, protecting the Grand Canyon from hydroelectric dams, and the regulation of workplace exposure to vinyl chloride—and found that none of them would have passed a conventional benefit-cost test.

COST-BENEFIT ANALYSIS, SUSTAINABILITY, AND THE ECONOMICS OF CLIMATE CHANGE

The potential problems raised by critics of standard CBA—incommensurability, irreversibility, uncertainty, non-marginal impacts—are magnified in the case of climate change. Before we examine the CBA of climate change, we should first look at how welfare economics is applied to the issue of sustainability. The conventional economic definition of sustainability is called **weak sustainability,** and it begins with the Walrasian welfare optimizing equation:

$$(8.1) \quad W(t) = \Sigma[C(t)] \, (1+r)^{-t}$$

where "total welfare" $W(t)$ is defined as per capita consumption over time $C(t)$ (total economic output) maximized over all feasible consumption paths $C(t)$. $W(t)$ is a broadly defined welfare function that includes both direct and indirect consumption, t is a specific time period, and r is the social discount rate. The economic or "weak" definition of intergenerational sustainability is:

$$(8.2) \quad dW(t) / dt \geq 0$$

A sustainable economy exhibits dynamic efficiency and a non-declining stream of social welfare over time. The problem of "sustainability" is reduced to allocating resources so as to smooth consumption over time. The **Hartwick–Solow rule** for weak sustainability is that an economy is sustainable if it maintains the capital stock necessary to sustain consumption over time. Capital stock is classified as either natural, manufactured, or **human capital,** as shown in Figure 8.1. The key assumption for weak sustainability is substitutability between the various kinds of capital. It is permissible (even desirable) to draw down **natural capital** and convert it to manufactured capital (converting a rain forest into a chain saw factory, for example) as long as this increases the discounted flow of economic output (per capita income). Again, the way the problem is framed in this system, the sole objective is to maximize the discounted flow of income over time.

There are many criticisms of this approach to sustainability. First, as we have seen, theoretical difficulties exist in determining whether a change in welfare, $dW(t)/dt$, is positive or negative using standard welfare methods. Second, equating the well-being of a society with per capita consumption is problematic (Frey and Stutzer 2002; Layard 2005). Third, ignoring the long-term biophysical requirements for sustainability is questionable. Finally, the standard welfare approach assumes commensurability. Biodiversity, climate stability, and all other features of the biophysical world are put on the same footing as ordinary market goods. Everything is substitutable and available for trade.

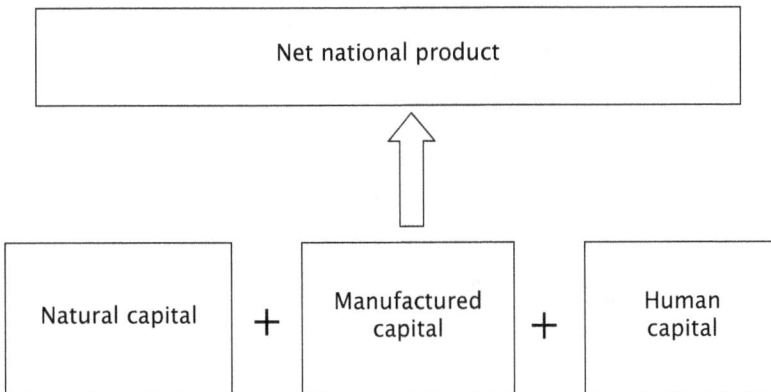

Figure 8.1. Weak sustainability

An alternative to weak sustainability is **strong sustainability,** which means sustaining the ability of natural capital (natural resources and the earth's life support systems) to maintain human activity. Strong sustainability is more difficult to define than weak sustainability, but it recognizes the need for public policy to regulate the ultimate sources of economic inputs (renewable and nonrenewable resources) and the flow of waste that are an inevitable result of economic activity (Daly 1977). The debate over global climate change, and policies to deal with it, has brought into sharp focus the complexity of the sustainability question and the weakness of the standard economic approach.

Climate Change Economics

A consensus has emerged among scientists and policy makers that global warming represents a major threat to the environment and to the well-being of humankind and the biosphere (Intergovernmental Panel on Climate Change 2007; Stern 2007). During the past century, the average global temperature has risen by about 1°C, with much of that increase due to fossil fuel burning and deforestation. The rate of increase has accelerated during the past twenty years or so as the human impact has begun to dominate natural processes. Global temperatures are projected to increase further by between 1.4°C and 5.8°C by 2100 and to continue to rise long after that. Scenarios of the likely consequences of such an increase differ substantially among regions but include sea level rise, shortages of fresh water, increased droughts and floods, more frequent and intense forest fires, more intense storms, more extreme heat episodes, agricultural disruption, the spread of infectious diseases, and biodiversity loss.

In October 2006, the British Treasury published the *Stern Review on the Economics of Climate Change* (Stern 2007). Because of the increasing urgency of the climate change issue, and the prestige of its lead author, the *Stern Review* received extensive press coverage and launched an ongoing debate about the role of economic analysis of issues involving very long time horizons and pure uncertainty. The release of the *Stern Review* may prove to be one of those pivotal events in intellectual history that provokes a sea change in the way a problem is framed and evaluated. At first the debate took place within the standard general equilibrium framework of contemporary economics and centered on the "proper" discount rate to apply to future costs and benefits of climate change mitigation. As the debate progressed, it became clear to many that there were more problems with the standard economic approach to climate change than the choice of a discount rate.

The most widely used economic models of climate change, including those of Nordhaus (1994) and Stern (2007) examine climate as a problem of allocating consumption over time within the weak sustainability framework discussed above. In economic jargon, a sustainable economy exhibits dynamic efficiency and a non-declining stream of maximized discounted social welfare over time. The rate at which future costs and benefits is discounted is determined by three parameters: the social rate of time preference (Δ), the **elasticity of consumption** (Δ), and the rate of growth of per capita consumption (g).

(8.3) $r = \Delta + \eta g$

Over long time periods, in the Walrasian framework, the estimated costs and benefits of climate change mitigation are driven by the choice of a discount rate. A low discount rate (as in Stern 2007) leads to cost-benefit results favoring immediate and substantial expenditures of resources on climate change mitigation. A higher discount rate (Nordhaus 1994) leads to cost-benefit results indicating that only moderate mitigation polices are needed. Within the standard climate change models the three components of r determine how responsible we are for decisions today that increase our well-being at the expense of future generations. The higher the discount rate, the less value we put on our negative impacts on those living in the future.

It is instructive to examine in detail the factors included in the discount rate in equation (8.3) and the arguments over their appropriate values. The rate of **pure time preference** (Δ) is a measure of the value of the well-being of future generations seen from the perspective of those living today. A positive value for Δ means that, all other things being equal, the farther into the future we go, the less the well-being of persons living there is worth to us. The higher the value of Δ, the less concerned we are about negative impacts in the future. A large literature exists arguing for a variety of different values for pure time preference, but it has become clear that there is no empirical way to determine the value of Δ. Choosing the rate of pure time preference comes down to a question of ethics, and there is scant evidence that the discussion about which discount rate to use has moved toward resolution over the last century. Ramsey (1928, 261) asserted eighty years ago that a positive rate of pure time preference was "ethically indefensible." On the other side of the debate, Pearce and colleagues (2003) took the position that a positive time discount rate is an observed fact because people do in fact discount the value of things expected to be received in the future. But even if we agree to use a market rate, which market rate should be used? Portney and Weyant (1999, 4) point out that "those looking for guidance on the choice of discount rate could find justification [in the literature] for a rate at or near zero, as high as 20 percent, and any and all values in between" (quoted in Cole 2008). Frederick, Loewenstein, and O'Donoghue (2004) report empirical estimates of discount rates ranging from −6 percent to 96,000 percent! Another objection is that U.S. market interest rates are typically used, but why should these rates be the norm? Climate change affects the entire world's population, including those from cultures with very different ideas about obligations to the future.

The other important factor in determining how much we should care about the future is how well off those in the future are likely to be. The standard economic model equates well-being with consumption and, as shown in equation (8.3), characterizes the material well-being of future generations using two components, the growth rate of per capita consumption in the future (g) and the elasticity of consumption (η). The elasticity of consumption shows the percentage change in well-being arising from a percentage change in the level of consumption. If η is equal to 1, corresponding to a logarithmic utility function, then 1 percent of today's income has the same value as 1 percent of income at some point in the future. So if per capita income today is $10,000 and income in the year 2100 is $100,000, $1,000 today has the same value as $10,000 in 2100. A $1,000 sacrifice today would be justified only if it added at least $10,000 to the average income of people living in the year 2100 (Quiggin 2007). The higher the value of η, the higher the future payoff must be for a sacrifice today. A number of assumptions are buried in the term η. For example, it is assumed that η is independent of the level or the growth rate of consumption.

A high value for η would seem to take the moral high ground—a given loss in income has a greater negative impact on a poor person than a rich person. A 10 percent loss of income to an impoverished person in Bangladesh is given more weight than a 10 percent income loss for a wealthy European. But if we assume, as most economic models do, that per capita consumption g continues to grow in the future, a higher η means a higher value for ηg and the less value we place on income losses for those in the future. Assuming a near-zero value for Δ and that $\eta = 1$ (as in Stern 2007) means that the discount rate (r) is determined by projections of the future growth rate of consumption, g.

The upshot over the sometimes heated debate over the value of the components of the discount rate, as described in equation (8.3), is that there is no objective, scientific answer to which particular values of these parameters should be used. Sound economic analysis is a combination of collecting and evaluating evidence and making explicit value judgments about that evidence.

CLIMATE CHANGE AND THE LIMITS
OF WALRASIAN ECONOMICS

The *Stern Review* moved economic analysis forward in several ways. First, it laid bare the arbitrariness of many of the assumptions buried in standard econometric models. Second, it brought to the forefront the ethical content of all economic models. Although most of the discussion of the *Stern Review* has centered on the economic modeling, most of the 700-page report discusses the science of climate change and the moral responsibility of humans toward the natural world and each other. Third, the *Stern Review* laid out in a clear and concise way the seriousness of the economic, biophysical, and social consequences of ignoring climate change.

The climate change debate has shown that the question of our obligation to future generations is a mater of ethics and best guesses as to the magnitude of the future consequences of climate change. This realization had led several prominent economists to question the ability of standard economic analysis to analyze problems involving the well-being of distant generations in the face of pure uncertainty and irreversible environmental changes. Quiggin (2007, 18) writes of the economic analysis of climate change: "The real difficulty here is that we are pushing economic analysis to its limits, in an area where fundamental problems, such as the equity premium puzzle [,] remain unresolved. Economists can help define the issues, but it is unlikely that economics can provide a final answer." Another leading environmental economist, Martin Weitzman, sees the *Stern Review* as "an opportunity for economists to take stock of what we know about this subject, how we know it, what we don't know, and why we don't know it" (Weitzman 2007a, 703).

The views of Quiggin and Weitzman suggest a significant reformulation of the role of economic analysis in the public policy debate. In the case of climate change, we are in a situation where the costs of mitigation may be large but the cost of inaction is potentially infinite, namely a catastrophic reorganization of the earth's climate and biosphere and the possible extinction of our species. It is likely that the magnitude of damages from the mega-greenhouse will be so great as to lie outside the marginal effects on GDP that have been the focus of traditional models. The Stern Review debate highlights the importance of recognizing the limits of standard science, not only economics, in dealing with situations involving large uncertainties about the possibility of catastrophic future events. In Weitzman's view, the economic analysis of global warming should be seen as a problem not of smoothing consumption over time but rather of determining how much insurance to provide to avoid a small chance of ruinous catastrophe.

COST-BENEFIT ANALYSIS AND THE EXPANSION
OF ECONOMIC THEORY AND POLICY

The above considerations do not imply that economic calculations of benefits and costs are unimportant. Nor do they imply that income is unimportant, or that only relative position matters, or that basic economic concepts such as opportunity costs, individual choice, and the importance of incentives are of no value. But as economists, we should pay more attention to our own admonishment that the starting point of analysis should be individual preferences. Assumptions about preferences and preference formation should be based on scientific evidence about how humans actually behave, not on expectations of how people *should* act in the stylized world of Walraisan general equilibrium theory. Economics is maturing rapidly as a science, and new theoretical developments and current empirical research should be incorporated in CBA. On this point there seems to be a convergence between mainstream economic theory and the more critical heterodox approaches. Hanley and Shogren (2005, 28) have expressed the need to incorporate contemporary experimental economics into cost-benefit analysis.

> Great value will exist, however, in developing a realistic yet formal behavioral underpinning for a revised CBA procedure/paradigm which relaxes the neoclassical straightjacket that has become uncomfortable for those who study environmental problems. This might be based on a more flexible, and therefore perhaps context-specific model of rational choice, where "rational" here means rational for both the individual operating within active and passive institutional contexts.

CBA was originally designed as a pragmatic way to examine real-world tradeoffs, not a universal blueprint to maximize social welfare in a general equilibrium framework. Specific government policies are most often formed within a limited frame of reference, for example, a municipality deciding whether or not to build a new bridge or road. These kinds of tradeoffs are not made against "everything else." Policy makers choose from a limited range of options, and the tradeoffs are made among those options. Many of the complicating issues discussed above can be safely ignored by a municipality deciding whether or not to build a bridge, a road, or a community center. This is

Traditional cost–benefit analysis

CBA of no use

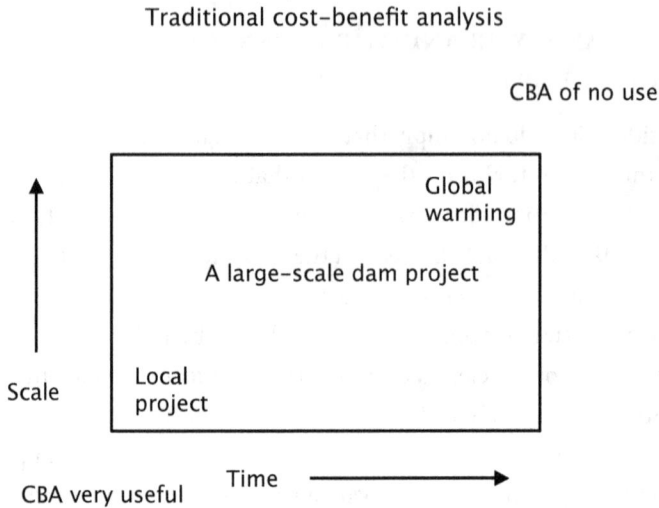

Figure 8.2. Cost-benefit analysis in time and space

a very different kind of decision than formulating policies to deal with the impacts of global climate change or worldwide biodiversity loss on future generations (Dasgupta 2008; Gowdy 2007).

As depicted in Figure 8.2, CBA is most useful for the kinds of cases for which it was first formulated, that is evaluating the benefits and costs of a specific local public project such as a new bridge. But within the envelope of Walrasian economics, CBA has become the way to look at everything from biodiversity loss to the effects of climate change a hundred years in the future. The Walrasian framework for CBA is not needed for small-scale projects where general equilibrium effects can be ignored and that framework is inappropriate as we broaden the scope of the analysis in time and space.

Cost-benefit analysis was considerably improved when non-market sources of well-being began to be considered in CBA estimates (Knetsch 2005). However, estimating non-pecuniary values uncovered many "anomalies" in preference formation including the WTA-WTP disparity, context-dependent valuation, lexicographic preferences, and so on. Policy analysts are now taking CBA to the next level by calling for more realistic assumptions about human behavior, human well-being, and preference formation. For example, Revesz and Livermore (2008) argue that the way CBA is usually framed makes it biased against regulations. It fails to account for the ability of the economy to adjust, so it overestimates costs. It also fails to adequately account for non-monetary values, so it underestimates benefits. Ackerman and Heinzerling (2004) also call for a more holistic method that incorporates moral sentiments, including prevailing notions of fairness and a precautionary approach to risk and uncertainty. Expanding CBA does not mean throwing out powerful, basic economic concepts developed over the last century. It does mean redefining and applying concepts such as "rational behavior," "social welfare," and "opportunity cost" using empirical evidence, ethical judgments, and sound scientific methods.

GLOSSARY

Contingent valuation—A valuation technique that uses surveys, interviews, and questionnaires to elicit values for things not traded in formal markets.

Elasticity of consumption—The percent change in well-being resulting in a small percentage increase in consumption.

Hartwick–Solow rule—Sustaining economic activity through time (ensuring non-declining consumption) depends upon maintaining the capital stock (natural, manufactured, and human capital) necessary to produce economic output.

Hedonic pricing—A valuation technique that uses market data to tease out implicit values for things that do not have specific market prices.

Human capital—The contribution to economic output arising from the stock of technical knowledge, cultural beliefs, habits, and institutions.

Incommensurability—In economic valuation, incommensurability refers to things that do not share a common standard of measure.

Loss aversion—The empirical finding that humans are willing to pay more to avoid the loss of something than they are to gain something they do not have.

Natural capital—The contribution to economic output arising from the services of the natural world and the stock of natural resources.

Precautionary principle—Policy makers should err on the side of caution when considering policies involving irreversibility and/or a large degree of uncertainty.

Pure time preference—In one sense it is a measure of an individual's impatience, that is, the degree to which a person would rather receive something now than in the future. In the context of inter-temporal policy decisions, it is a measure of how much we discount the utility of a person living in the future compared with that of a person living today.

Strong sustainability—Sustaining the life-support systems of planet earth that are the ultimate source of human well-being.

Subjective well-being—A measure of a person's self-perceived level of well-being.

Weak sustainability—The economic definition of sustainability, that is, sustaining economic output or per capita income through time.

REFERENCES AND FURTHER READING

Ackerman, F., and L. Heinzerling. 2004. *Priceless: On Knowing the Price of Everything and the Value of Nothing.* New York: The New Press.

Bromley, D. 1990. The ideology of efficiency: Searching for a theory of policy analysis. *Journal of Environmental Economics and Management* 19, 86–107.

Brown, T., and R. Gregory. 1999. Why the WTA-WTP disparity matters. *Ecological Economics* 28, 323–335.

Cole, D. 2008. The *Stern Review* and its critics: Implications for the theory and practice of benefit-cost analysis. *Natural Resources Journal* 48, 53–90.

Daly, H. E. 1977. *Steady State Economics.* San Francisco: W. H. Freeman.

Dasgupta, P. 2008. Nature in economics. *Environmental and Resource Economics* 39, 1–7.

Easterlin, R. 1974. Does economic growth improve the human lot? Some empirical evidence. In P. David and M. Reder (eds.), *Nations and Happiness in Economic Growth: Essays in Honor of Moses Abramowitz.* New York: Academic Press, 89–125.

Frederick, S., G. Loewenstein, and T. O'Donoghue. 2004. Time discounting and time preference: A critical review. In C. Camerer, G. Lowenstein, and

M. Rabin (eds.), *Advances in Behavioral Economics*. Princeton, NJ: Princeton University Press, 162–222.

Frey, B., and A. Stutzer. 2002. *Happiness and Economics: How the Economy and Institutions Affect Well-Being*. Princeton, NJ: Princeton University Press.

Gintis, H. 2000. Beyond *Homo economicus*: Evidence from experimental economics. *Ecological Economics* 35, 311–322.

Gowdy, J. 2004. The revolution in welfare economics and its implications for environmental valuation and policy. *Land Economics* 80, 239–257.

Gowdy, J. 2007. Toward an experimental basis for benefit-cost analysis. *Ecological Economics* 63, 649–655.

Hanley, N., and J. Shogren. 2005. Is cost-benefit analysis anomaly proof? *Environmental and Resource Economics* 32, 13–34.

Intergovernmental Panel on Climate Change. 2007. *Climate Change 2007: The Physical Science Basis*. Contribution of Working Group I to the Fourth Assessment Report of the Intergovernmental Panel on Climate Change, Geneva, Switzerland. Available at http://www.ipcc.ch.

Knetsch, J. 2005. Gains, losses, and the US-EPA *Economic Analyses Guidelines*: A hazardous product. *Environmental & Resource Economics* 32, 91–112.

Laibson, D. 1997. Golden eggs and hyperbolic discounting. *Quarterly Journal of Economics* 112, 443–477.

Layard, R. 2005. *Happiness: Lessons from a New Science*. New York: Penguin Books.

Nordhaus, W. 1994. *Managing the Global Commons: The Economics of Climate Change*. Cambridge, MA: MIT Press.

Pearce, D., G. Atkinson, and S. Mourato. 2006. *Cost-Benefit Analysis and the Environment*. Paris: OECD.

Pearce, D., B. Groom, C. Hepburn, and P. Koundori. 2003. Valuing the future: Recent advances in social discounting. *World Economics* 4(2), 121–141.

Portney, P., and J. Weyant. 1999. Introduction. In P. R. Portney and J. P. Weyant (eds.), *Discounting and Intergenerational Equity*. Washington, DC: Resources for the Future, 1–11.

Quiggin, J. 2007. Stern and the critics on discounting. Mimeo, University of Queensland.

Ramsey, F. 1928. A mathematical theory of saving. *Economic Journal* 38, 543–549.

Revesz, R., and M. Livermore. 2008. *Rethinking Rationality: How Cost-Benefit Analysis Can Better Protect the Environment and Our Health.* New York: Oxford University Press.

Spash, C. 2007. Deliberative monetary valuation (DMV): Issues in combining economic and political processes to value environmental change. *Ecological Economics* 63, 690–700.

Stern, N. 2007. *The Economics of Climate Change: The Stern Review.* Cambridge: Cambridge University Press.

Stigler, G., and G. Becker. 1977. De gustibus non est disputandum. *American Economic Review* 67, 76–90.

Weitzman, M. 1998. Why the far distant future should be discounted at the lowest possible rate. *Journal of Environmental Economics and Management* 36, 201–208.

Weitzman, M. 2007a. A review of the *Stern Review on the Economics of Climate Change. Journal of Economic Literature* 45, 703–724.

Weitzman, M. 2007b. On modeling and interpreting the economics of catastrophic climate change. Memo, December 5.

Willig, R. 1976. Consumers' surplus without apology. *American Economic Review* 66, 589–597.

9

THE FUTURE OF ECONOMIC
THEORY AND POLICY

> Only economists still put the cart before the horse by claiming that
> the growing turmoil of mankind can be eliminated if prices are
> right. The truth is that only if our values are right will prices also be
> so. We had to introduce progressive taxation, social security, and
> strict rules for forest exploitation, and now we struggle with
> anti-pollution laws, precisely because the market mechanism by
> itself can never heal a wrong.
> —*Nicholas Georgescu-Roegen,* Energy and Economic Myths *(New York:
> Pergamon Press, 1976), xix*

PUBLIC POLICY IN THE WALRASIAN SYSTEM

The theoretical controversies discussed in previous chapters may seem esoteric to most non-economists and even to many economists. But the power of
the formalization of Adam Smith's invisible hand in neoclassical welfare
theory has driven economic policy in the decades since World War II. The
antipathy to public policy is reflected in the language of most economics textbooks. For example, policies to protect the environment are characterized
as either "command and control" or "free-market" solutions. Who would
want to be commanded and controlled when they could be free? But today the
theoretical and empirical challenges to the Walrasian model are beginning to
spill over into the realm of public policy.

Decades of theoretical work has shown that, even if we grant all the restrictive assumptions of welfare economics, from *Homo economicus* to perfectly operating competitive markets, there is no way to "close" the neoclassical welfare system from within. There is no way to pick a particular Pareto
optimal distribution without appealing to an ethical judgment (Bowles and
Gintis 2000; Chipman and Moore 1978; Suzumura 1999). The potential Pareto

improvement (PPI) principle was promoted as an alternative to the social welfare function, which could be constructed only by making interpersonal comparisons of utility. But the PPI approach foundered on the assumption that preferences are independent and additive rather than interactive. The search for a **positive economics** free of value judgments turned out to be an exercise in futility. Turning policy decisions over to the market is as much an ethical judgment as any other public policy.

The mathematical constraints of the Walrasian system dictate that there can be no interaction between economic agents, whether they are producers or consumers, and no interaction between "the market" and the social and biophysical systems ultimately supporting all economic activity. There is an artificial separation between the market and the rest of the world. This world-view drives the policy recommendations of most economists. The standard view of the role of economic policy falls directly out of the view of the economy as a self-contained circular flow, as depicted in Figure 9.1.

Within this self-referential system, the policy goal is to maximize the utility individuals get from consuming market goods. Social welfare is the additive sum of the utility of all the individuals in society, so that when all the individuals maximize their utility, subject to the resources at their disposal,

Figure 9.1. Walrasian theory depicts a self-contained system sealed off from nature and society

the social optimum is achieved. Given that free exchange of commodities and inputs leads to the best possible outcome, the role of government is limited to policies that expand the scope of the market. Prominent among these policies is expanding trade, which brings more consumers and firms into the system to provide more choices. Another favored policy is to bring more activity into the market by taking it from the public sphere through deregulation and privatization. If pollution, biodiversity loss, or climate change are recognized as problems, this is an indication that they need to be brought into the Walrasian market economy by assigning property rights to them. All problems are solved by bringing market forces into action.

The Walrasian model has been consciously used to dismiss any sort of cooperative, collective public policy. Only by ensuring that prices are "correct" and that property rights are fully specified can free-riding and inefficiency be vanquished. Economic efficiency receives priority over "messy" public discourse. According to Milton Friedman (1962, 24):

> The wider the range of activities covered by the market, the fewer are issues on which explicitly political decisions are required and hence on which it is necessary to achieve agreement. In turn, the fewer the issues on which agreement is necessary, the greater is the likelihood of getting agreement while maintaining a free society.

Daniel Bromley (2007, 677) describes the takeover of public discourse by the let-the-market-decide mentality:

> Democracy as public participation and reasoned discourse is somehow suspect—not to be trusted. It seems that the public's business cannot be properly conducted unless it adheres to the precepts of individualistic models of "rational choice" applied to collective action. . . . It is a quest for public policy in which applied microeconomics is deployed as the only way to impose "rationality" on an otherwise incoherent and quite untrustworthy political process.

But in the last decade or so, the well-publicized failures of laissez-faire economics have led a growing number of economists to recognize the limits of market outcomes as the ultimate manifestation of the common good. This is not to dispute the fact that market-based policies such as trade agreements may indeed increase social welfare or that putting prices on features of the natural world will help society to understand their true value. However, such policies should be based on real-world experience and the observed behavior of actual humans, not on systems of equations describing how consumers and firms in an abstract ideal world *should* behave.

A REALISTIC CONCEPTION OF THE ECONOMIC PROCESS

As illustrated in Figure 9.1, the Walrasian economy is independent of nature and society. The alternative view is that all economic activity is framed by human institutions and completely dependent upon inputs from nature. Figure 9.2 shows the economy as a one-way flow of inputs from nature transformed by the economic process and reentering the natural world as dissipated matter and energy.

Figure 9.2 shows the economy not as a self-contained circular flow but rather a one-way process limited by the laws of **thermodynamics.** The first law of thermodynamics states that energy cannot be created or destroyed; the second law (the **entropy law**) states that energy is continually degraded from an organized form (low entropy) to an disorganized form (high entropy). For example, if someone burns a lump of coal in a sealed room, the same amount of heat energy is present in the room but it can no longer be harnessed for useful work. The human economy is dependent on flows of low-entropy energy (and raw materials) entering the system to be degraded and discharged

The Resource Base   Firms   Households   Resource Sinks

Figure 9.2. The economy as an evolving thermodynamic system

as high-entropy waste (Georgescu-Roegen 1971). This conceptualization of the economic process is summarized by Robert Ayres (2008, 17–18):

> We conceptualize the economic system as a multi-sector chain of linked processing stages, starting with resource extraction, reduction, refining, conversion, production of finished goods and services (including capital goods), final consumption (and disposal of wastes). Each stage has physical inputs and physical outputs that pass to the next stage. At each stage of processing value is added and useful information is embodied in the products, while low value, high entropy, low information wastes are separated and disposed of. Global entropy increases at every step, of course, but the value-added process tends to reduce the entropy of useful products, while increasing the entropy of the wastes.

Based on the entropy law, and what we have seen so far about the social nature of production and consumption, the system depicted in Figure 9.2 highlights the following features of a modern industrial economy: (1) economic activity is totally dependent on low-entropy inputs from the natural resource base, (2) firms are social institutions that transform energy and matter into economically valuable products, (3) consumers "consume" the services of these products within a socially constructed and ever-changing system of preferences, and (4) the ultimate output of the economy is high-entropy waste discarded back into the natural world. This way of looking at the economy suggests very different policy approaches compared with the self-contained circular flow model depicted in Figure 9.1.

POLICIES FOR THE RESOURCE BASE

In the Walrasian world, the role of natural resources as critical productive inputs is either downplayed or ignored completely. As we saw in Chapter 2, in this system all inputs enter the trading system on an equal footing and all are substitutable for one another. In perfectly functioning markets there is no need for polices to deal with resource scarcity. As Solow (1974, 11) puts it in an oft-quoted remark: "If it is very easy to substitute other factors for natural resources, then there is, in principle, no problem. The world can, in effect, get along without natural resources." To be fair, Solow is more careful than most economists in his statement by using the word "if." But the question remains:

What "other factors" of production can substitute for natural resources so that we can get along without them? Capital is a physical construct made by using energy and labor to combine raw materials into machines of various kinds. The pool of labor is a collection of human beings whose bodies are made up of combinations of elements from the periodic table. Humans, like other living species, maintain themselves by extracting a steady supply of oxygen, water, and minerals from natural world. Even the amorphous ingredient technology must be applied to some physical objects.

In the Walrasian system the choice of productive inputs is driven by relative prices—as prices go up, substitutes are found. All scarcity is relative, not absolute. Referring to the Edgeworth box diagram in Chapter 2 (Figure 2.2), suppose that the labor force (L) is reduced by one-half. This would change only the slope of the isoquants, but it would not change the ability of the economy to achieve an efficient allocation of inputs. Given the new endowments of labor and capital, and an initial distribution of them, a unique Pareto-efficient combination of K and L would still be generated by the free trade of inputs. There is always a market clearing price consistent with an equilibrium supply and demand of any input. But this says nothing about what the effect of such a loss of labor would be on a real economy. Within the confines of the Edgeworth box, debates as to the importance of specific inputs are confined to questions about the elasticity of substitution of those inputs relative to some other input or aggregation of inputs.

In a more encompassing and dynamic view of the economy there is ample reason to worry about the ability of the market to foresee the consequences of resource constraints. This is especially true of fossil fuel energy. One barrel of oil contains the equivalent of roughly 23,000 hours of human work output (see the calculation of this by David Pimentel at http://www.lifeaftertheoilcrash .net/Research.html#anchor_71). The fossil fuel bonanza, and the resulting increase in the ability to do useful work, revolutionized the human economy in the twentieth century. But according to the entropy law, the passage of fossil fuel through the economy is a one-way trip. Concentrated energy is drawn from the earth, used to power the economy, and discharged as dissipated heat and other by-products such as carbon dioxide. As we saw in our discussion of the Cobb–Douglas production function in Chapter 2, economists tend to attribute the phenomenal increase in economic output since the beginning of the twentieth century to technology. This is calculated as total factor productivity, a "residual" left over in growth accounting after calculating the contribution of productive inputs.

Ayres and Warr (2005) found that all standard constant returns to scale production function models fail to explain the 100-year growth history of the U.S. economy without introducing a "technology" multiplier. But they also found that most improvements in technology have been simply an increase in **exergy,** that is, energy calculated as useful physical work. Similar results were found by Hall, Cleveland, and Kaufmann (1986). Their work indicates that the fossil fuel bonanza of the last hundred years or so explains the phenomenal growth in economic output during that period. The recent (2008) spike in energy prices, and the stagnation in the growth of world petroleum production, has underscored the critical importance of energy in modern economic growth. This importance has taken on a new urgency with the warning from prominent petroleum analysts (for example, Simons 2005) that we are at or near the peak production of the world's oil supply. After this peak we can expect a sharply decreasing efficiency in petroleum extraction in terms of the physical requirements for obtaining additional supplies.

Viewing the economy as an evolving system dependent upon the flow of services from the natural world suggests a need for explicit and proactive energy policies. Such policies should be undertaken with an understanding of how they impact the other stages of the system depicted in Figure 9.2. Resource policies might restrict and/or redirect the use of some scarce resources (such as fossil fuels) in order to allow more time to develop substitutes or to switch to a less intensive use of these resources in production and consumption. In a linear view of the economy, policies would recognize the long-term evolutionary potential and requirements of the human economy, the impact of patterns of resource use on human institutions (Diamond 2005; Tainter 1995; Tainter Allen, and Hoelstra 2006), and the impact of resource extraction on the living world that supports all human life. Such an approach would recognize the physical limits to resource extraction and the importance of qualitative changes in the resource base.

There are ways to measure the increasing scarcity of energy. One measure is the energy return on energy invested (**EROEI**), which shows how much energy can be obtained from the expenditure of a unit of energy. In the 1930s, the EROI for U.S. oil was about 100:1 but it has declined to somewhere around 17:1 in 2003 (Hall et al. 2003, 320). This is still a highly favorable investment (as is investment in energy from wind and coal), but this means that our subsidy from nature has declined dramatically in recent decades and is likely to decline even more sharply in the future. Again, a proactive approach to increasing energy scarcity calls for policies to smooth the transition to a less energy-intensive economy.

THE FIRM AS A SOCIAL INSTITUTION

The role of the firm in the economy has long been a matter of debate. As we saw earlier, Walrasian theory was first developed to describe consumer behavior. The equations were then simply relabeled to create a model of production (see the discussion in Mirowski 1989, chapter 5). As the quote by Léon Walras at the beginning of Chapter 2 suggests, there was no apparent role for the firm to play. With the consumer as utility-maximizing rational economic man at the center of economic analysis, there was no obvious ultimate reason for the firm to exist in the simple barter model. Why is it in the firm's interest to supply goods to consumers? The question of why firms exist was taken up in the 1930s by Coase (1937), who proposed that the purpose of the firm was to lower the cost of "discovering prices," that is, to minimize transactions costs in production. This led naturally to the elaboration of the role of the firm as a cost-minimizing vehicle to make a profit by satisfying the preferences of consumers. The marketing literature shows the strong influence of Walrasian economic theory. Customers are perceived as "economic men" with stable and well-defined tastes waiting to be uncovered by marketing research and satisfied by efficient production techniques. As a well-known marketing text puts it:

> In its fullest sense, the marketing concept is a philosophy of business which states that the customer's want satisfaction is the economic and social justification of a company's existence. Consequently, all company activities in production, engineering and finance, as well as in marketing, must be devoted first to determining what the customer's wants are and then to satisfying those wants while still making a reasonable profit. (Wilmhurst 1978)

If the goal of human society is to satisfy consumer preferences in the most efficient way possible, then any deviation on the part of the firm from the goal of profit maximization through efficient resource allocation is not only unjustified but also detrimental to the public good. In Friedman's words (1962, 133): "In a free economy there is one and only one social responsibility of business—to use its resources and engage in activities designed to increase its profits so a long as it stays within the rules of the game, which is to say, engages in open and free competition."

If we step outside the Walrasian optimizing framework and take a broader view of the firm as a highly evolved social institution (Cordes et al. 2008), what are the implications for economic theory and policy?

There Is No Single "Best" Way for a Firm to Operate

The idea that there is a single, optimal level of profit, wages, and prices for a firm is part of the ideology of Walrasian economics. It is teleological in its belief that perfect competition, with prices corrected for market failure, leads not only to equilibrium but also to the equilibrium of Pareto efficiency. The end result of perfect competition is not merely one of many possibilities. It is the optimal outcome—the best of all possible worlds—because it is based on the sovereign preferences of consumers. If a firm does not strive to maximize profit, it is actually acting against the best interest of society in the sense that it is reducing potential economic output, the one true source of social welfare. In reality, there is no precise, single, optimal outcome to strive for. A wide range of sales, employment, and profit strategies, spanning the very short term to the very long term, are consistent with "rational" firm behavior. Many strategies are available to a firm, and each one is associated with an array of social relationships and obligations.

New theories of the firm are being developed based on Herbert Simon's notion of **satisficing** and the recognition of **bounded rationality.** According to Simon (1987), the modern firm may be obligated to achieve some satisfactory level of profit, but then it is free to pursue other goals. Bounded rationality recognizes that Walrasian rationality is limited by the evolved characteristics of human cognition. These evolved traits include cooperative behavior, the use of heuristics and rules of thumb in decision making, and a variety of behaviors to control free-riding and foster cooperation. An early challenge to the rationalist view of the firm came from the work of Cyert and March (1963), who argued that organizations fall back on standardized decision rules, or rules of thumb, such as standard operating procedures and markup pricing. Nelson and Winter (1982) developed an evolutionary theory of the firm based on the generation, selection, and retention of "routines," that is, effective packages of technologies and organizational practices.

The Modern Corporation Is a Complex, Evolving Institution with Many Public as Well as Purely Economic Goals

Cordes et al. (2008) point out that the firm is the quintessential cooperative venture. Firms that are able to harness the tendency to cooperate can capture benefits that are not feasible through market incentives alone. Firms are also culturally variable and can evolve new forms of organization and new purposes as social (and environmental) conditions change. This is important to keep in mind as new requirements for firms emerge in the light of climate change and increasing energy scarcity. Firms are much more adaptable and proactive than standard theory tells us. Related to this is the work of Witt (1998, 2005) who argues that successful entrepreneurs build on the human capacity for group beneficial behavior.

It may be true that the ultimate purpose of the firm is to satisfy consumer demand. But as Georgescu-Roegen (1976, 9) pointed out, the ultimate purpose of consumption is not obtaining physical objects of production but rather an "immaterial flux—the enjoyment of life." Firms ultimately provide services rather than physical products. This observation has important implications for reducing the need for physical objects (cars and appliances, for example). (Ayres 2008).

Consumers' enjoyment of products may include positive or negative feelings about how they are made, their effects on the environment, and their place within a given social and ethical system. The **corporate social responsibility** movement is based on this idea. Although corporations are much more structurally constrained by material self-interest, in the form of profits for shareholders, even they are not immune to social norms that are increasingly defining and demanding responsible and fair behavior, with punishment of violators common (Kahneman, Knetsch, and Thaler 1986). However, as

Zamagni (1995, xx) suggests: "Since a market economy gives people differentially strong incentives to act on their various preferences (and generally none at all to act on altruistic preferences), measures should be taken at the institutional level to avoid that those individuals, whose conceptions require behavior that cuts against the selfishness logic, result in being heavily penalized." Policies designed solely on the basis of self-interested behavior may crowd out behaviors that promote the pubic good (Bowles 2008). The specifics of this dynamic and the coevolution of corporate social behavior and society in general deserve more investigation.

CONSUMERS AS HUMANS

Standard theory assumes that utility (happiness or well-being) can be equated with the ability to consume market goods and services (or money income). In recent years macroeconomic polices have focused almost exclusively on increasing total gross domestic product (GDP). As we saw in Chapter 8, recent research in well-being and happiness implies that the near-exclusive policy focus on GDP growth as a means to increase social welfare may be misplaced. Increased consumption does not lead automatically to increased welfare. In light of this, Kahneman, Wakker, and Sarin (1997) suggest going back to the roots of economics and defining "welfare" as "the greatest good for the greatest number," as **Jeremy Bentham** suggested. According to Ng (1999), current measures of **subjective utility** make us closer than ever imagined to developing something like Bentham's "hedonometer" to provide a cardinal measure of utility. Methods have been devised, tested, and calibrated to accurately measure levels of happiness across individuals and even across cultures (Ferrer-i-Carbonell and Frijters 2004; Frey and Stutzer 2002, 21). The existence of scientific measures of well-being, together with an increasing array of other social, environmental, and economic indicators, makes it possible to formulate economic policies that directly enhance social welfare.

Psychologists have long argued that well-being comes from a wide variety of individual, social, and genetic factors. Surveys, behavioral experiments, and neurological analysis have identified key factors positively influencing well-being. These include health (especially self-reported health), close relationships and marriage, intelligence, education, and religion (Ferrer-i-Carbonell and van Praag 2002; Frey and Stutzer 2002). Age, gender, and income also influence happiness but not to the degree once thought. Some regularities in the relationship between income and happiness have been established. First, people in wealthier countries are generally happier than people in poorer countries (Diener, Diener, and Diener, 1995). But even this correlation is weak, and the happiness data shows many anomalies. For example, some surveys show that people in Nigeria are happier than people in Austria, France, and Japan (Frey and Stutzer 2002, table 2.2, 35). Second, past a certain stage of development, increasing incomes do not lead to greater happiness. For example, real per capita income in the United States has increased sharply in recent decades but reported happiness has declined (Blanchflower and Oswald 2000). Similar results have been reported for Japan and Western Europe (Easterlin 1995). Studies of individuals also show a lack of correlation between increases in income and increases in happiness (Frey and Stutzer 2002). Third, security seems to be a key element in happiness. Large welfare gains would come from a focus on improving welfare based on those things that increase individual security, such as health insurance, old-age security, employment, and job security. Fourth, mental health is a crucial factor in happiness. Frey and Stutzer (2002) and Layard (2005) argue, based on happiness survey results, for more public spending on mental health, especially for the very young because apparently the first few years of a person's life play a large role in their future happiness. If we want future generations to experience a high and sustainable level of welfare, we are likely to get high rates of return by investing in policies to ensure adequate child nutrition, health care, education, and family counseling. Fifth, richer social relationships generally make people happier. This implies that welfare gains may be obtained from policies promoting increased leisure time and more public spending on social and recreational infrastructure.

Economists are beginning to reconsider the role of public policy in promoting the social good (Bowles 2008; Frey 1997). Frank (1999) suggests that our beliefs about human nature help shape human nature itself and that the self-interest paradigm can be self-fulfilling. He used Prisoner's Dilemma experiments that showed that students tended to be less cooperative after taking just one semester of traditional microeconomics: "The exposed subjects come to perceive self-interest as a normative characterization of rational behavior and to act accordingly." Zamagni (1995, xx) suggests that the "self-interest bias" in economic policy requires that we "redress this imbalance by fostering or creating institutions that encourage a commitment to social goals."

POLICES FOR ENVIRONMENTAL SUSTAINABILITY

In recent decades, concern about the relationship between economic activity and the natural world has focused more and more on environmental sustainability, that is, the effect of economic production on the earth's life-support systems. Two of the most important environmental effects of global economic activity are biodiversity loss and climate change. Climate change, as discussed in Chapter 8, has the potential to have devastating effects on the earth's life-support systems and human well-being. The predicted effects of climate change are quite dire if we continue with a business-as-usual approach to economic growth and fossil fuel use. The related problem of biodiversity loss also has the potential to greatly diminish human well-being. Biodiversity loss will almost certainly accelerate due to the effects of climate change.

According to most ecologists, the current loss of biological diversity amounts to the sixth major extinction episode in the estimated 600-million-year existence of complex life on planet Earth. In what is still one of the most thorough surveys to date, Pimm et al. (1995) estimated that the current rate of extinction is 100 to 1,000 times the background rate and accelerating. What is the value of nature and why should we preserve it (Norton, 1986)? In regard to biodiversity, we may distinguish three hierarchies of value and three meanings of sustainability: economic, social, and ecological (Gowdy 1997).

The Economic Value of Biodiversity

In Chapter 8 we examined the standard economic view of sustainability, weak sustainability, meaning a non-declining growth of per capita GDP (or more precisely Hicksian income). Weak sustainability is ensured by maintaining the total capital stock necessary to produce consumption goods, assuming the substitutability between natural, manufactured, and human capital. Economists do recognize the importance of biodiversity to the human economy. Ecotourism, the importance of genetic diversity in maintaining the health of agriculture, bio-prospecting for medicinal plants, and many other contributions of nature to the economy have been documented by economists. Perhaps the most ambitious attempt to value the services of nature was that of Costanza et al. (1997), who systematically inventoried of the value several types of ecosystem services. Of course, placing monetary values on biodiversity within the traditional economics framework runs into the theoretical difficulties inherent in discounting, marginal valuation, and identifying potential Pareto improvements.

The Social Value of Biodiversity

As we have seen earlier, individual preferences cannot be fully captured in the narrow realm of market exchange. In the case of biodiversity loss, we are dealing with irreversibility, very long-term scales, and unknowable consequences. Humans apparently have a deep psychological need for interaction with nature (what E. O. Wilson [1984] calls "biophilia"). Interaction with nature as been found to be beneficial in a variety of forms, from the production benefits of having live plants in offices to the physical and mental benefits of Outward Bound trips to the medicinal benefits of pets in nursing homes.

Including nonmarket and probably unmeasurable values of biodiversity brings us into the realm of strong sustainability, mentioned in Chapter 8. Strong sustainability is not well-defined but it means sustaining the earth's life-support systems and ensuring a stable and equitable socioeconomic system. It recognizes that sustainability is not only an economic problem but also a problem of maintaining essential, irreplaceable, and non-substitutable environmental features (Ayres 2008). This is sometimes referred to as **critical natural capital** (Farley 2008).

The Ecological Value of Biodiversity

As we saw in the case of climate change, the earth's natural systems work by different rules than markets do. The timescales are frequently very long—in the cases of climate change and biodiversity that may be tens of thousands of years or even longer. Individual species, including humans, are expendable to maintain the stability of ecosystems. Diverse ecosystems seem to be more resilient to environmental disturbances (Tilman and Downing 1994). As biodiversity is lost, so too is the evolutionary potential to adapt to inevitable environmental changes. The total ecosystem value of biodiversity may be the value of the existence of humans and all other species.

CONCLUSION

Within the economics profession, there is a growing clash of worldviews between those who view the human future as a mechanical unfolding of rational choice through market expansion and those who advocate a reasoned public debate about how to make the world a better place (Bowles 2008; Bromley 2007). The following could serve as a guide for evaluating long-term economic policies.

1. Standard economic analysis evaluates the future in terms of the present, as in "discounted present value." However, the approach should be to consider the present in terms of the future. What would people in the future like for us to do now so that their world might be a better place? Such an approach recognizes the limits to substitution and employs the precautionary principle rather than the optimization principle.

From this it follows that:

2. Present polices should avoid future lock-in to the greatest extent possible. Irreversible changes should be avoided where possible.
3. Present polices should be flexible enough to allow for rapid adaptation to changing conditions.
4. Policies in the present should enhance the ability of persons in the future to control their own destinies. This should mean much more than just increasing total income (or the income of a representative agent).
5. Focusing on pecuniary motivations alone ignores the richness of human motivation and may be ineffective or even counterproductive.

This is an exciting time to be studying economics. The profession is in the middle of a paradigm shift and the field will look very different ten years from now. It is a formidable task to construct economic policy scenarios based on the new ideas now dominating theoretical and policy discussions. But even a relatively simple and transparent analysis of present problems and possible solutions is much more useful than the standard general equilibrium consumption-smoothing model with its layers of arbitrary assumptions.

GLOSSARY

Bounded rationality—The idea that limited cognitive ability, or cognitive blinders, prevents people from seeking and using available information. There are bounds to human rationality.

Corporate social responsibility—The idea that businesses should recognize the interests of society by taking responsibility for the impact of their activities on the larger community and on the environment. This includes improving the quality of life for employees and their families as well as for consumers of the product.

Critical natural capital—Features of the natural world that generate benefits to humans and that have few if any substitutes.

Entropy law—Energy is continually degraded from an organized form (low entropy) to a disorganized form (high entropy) (this is the second law of thermodynamics).

EROEI—Acronym for energy return on energy invested. The amount of direct and indirect energy required to obtain a unit of energy.

Exergy—Energy used calculated as the efficiency of getting it to the point where the work is done.

Jeremy Bentham (1748–1832)—English philosopher and social reformer considered to be the father of utilitarianism, that is, the moral worth of an action is solely determined by its effect upon the well-being calculated as the sum of happiness of all persons.

Positive economics—The idea that economics can be a value-free science in that it describes "what is" rather than "what ought to be."

Satisficing—People and firms do the best they can with limited information and limited cognitive ability to achieve multiple objectives. It is opposed to the idea that economic agents attempt to maximize a single objective function.

Subjective utility—Utility expressed in terms of an individual's personal judgment or degree of satisfaction rather than by preferences as revealed in market outcomes.

Thermodynamics—The first law of thermodynamics states that energy cannot be created or destroyed. The second law (the entropy law) states that, in a closed system, energy is continually degraded from an organized form (low entropy) to a disorganized form (high entropy).

REFERENCES AND FURTHER READING

Biodiversity

Costanza, R., R. d'Arge, R. de Groot, S. Farber, M. Grasso, B. Hannon, K. Limburg, S. Naeem, R. O'Neill, J. Paruelo, R. Raskin, P. Sutton, and M. van der Belt. 1997. The value of the world's ecosystem services and natural capital. *Nature* 387, 253–260.

Farley, J. 2008. The role of prices in conserving critical natural capital. *Conservation Biology* 22(6), 1399–1408.

Gowdy, J. 1997. The value of biodiversity. *Land Economics* 73, 25–41.

Norton, B. 1986. *Why Preserve Natural Variety?* Princeton, NJ: Princeton University Press.

Pimm, S., G. Russel, J. Gittleman, and T. Brooks. 1995. The future of biodiversity. *Science* 269, 347–350.

Tilman, D., and J. Downing. 1994. Biodiversity and stability in grasslands. *Nature* 367, 363–365.

Wilson, E. O. 1984. *Biophilia*. Cambridge, MA: Harvard University Press.

Energy

Ayres, R., and D. Warr. 2005. Accounting for growth: The role of physical work. *Cultural Change and Economic Dynamics* 16, 211–220.

Georgescu-Roegen, N. 1971. *The Entropy Law and the Economic Process.* Cambridge, MA: Harvard University Press.

Georgescu-Roegen, N. 1976. *Energy and Economic Myths.* New York: Pergamon Press.

Hall, C., C. Cleveland, and R. Kaufmann. 1986. *Energy and Resource Quality: The Ecology of the Economic Process.* New York: Wiley Interscience.

Hall, C., P. Tharakan, J. Hallock, C. Cleveland, and M. Jefferson. 2003. Hydrocarbons and the evolution of human culture. *Nature* 426(6964), 318–322.

Simons, M. 2005. *Twilight in the Desert.* New York: Wiley.

Neoclassical Critiques

Bowles, S., and H. Gintis. 2000. Walrasian economics in retrospect. *Quarterly Journal of Economics* 115, 1411–1439.

Chipman, J., and J. Moore. 1978. The new welfare economics 1939–1974. *International Economic Review* 19, 547–584.

Colander, D. 2000. The death of neoclassical economics. *Journal of the History of Economic Thought* 22, 127–143.

Mirowski, P. 1989. *More Heat than Light.* Cambridge: Cambridge University Press.

Private Versus Social Incentives

Bowles, S. 2008. Policies designed for self-interested citizens may undermine "The Moral Sentiments": Evidence from economic experiments. *Science* 320, 1605–1609.

Frank, R. 1999. *Luxury Fever: Why Money Fails to Satisfy in an Age of Excess.* New York: Free Press.

Frey, B. 1997. A constitution of knaves crowds out civic virtues. *Economic Journal* 107, 1043–1053.

Social Choice

Bromley, D. 2007. Environmental regulations and the problem of sustainability: Moving beyond "market failure." *Ecological Economics* 63, 676–683.

Kahneman, D., J. L. Knetsch, and R. Thaler. 1986. Fairness as a constraint on profit seeking: Entitlements in the market. *American Economic Review* 76, 728–741.

Suzumura, K. 1999. Paretian welfare judgments and Bergsonian social choice. *Economic Journal* 109, 204–221.

Societal Evolution

Diamond, J. 2005. *Collapse: How Societies Choose to Fail or Succeed.* New York: Viking.

Hall, C., P. Tharakan, J. Hallock, C. Cleveland, and M. Jefferson. 2003. Hydrocarbons and the evolution of human culture. *Nature* 426(6964), 318–322.

Tainter, J. 1995. Sustainability of complex societies. *Futures* 97, 397–407.

Tainter, J., T. Allen, and T. Hoelstra. 2006. Energy transformations and post-normal science. *Energy* 31, 44–58.

Subjective Utility and Well-Being

Blanchflower, D., and D. Oswald. 2000. Well-being over time in Britain and the U.S.A. NBER Working Paper 7481. Cambridge, MA: National Bureau of Economic Analysis.

Diener, E., M. Diener, and C. Diener. 1995. Factors predicting the well-being of nations. *Journal of Personality and Social Psychology* 69, 851–864.

Easterlin, R. 1974. Does economic growth improve the human lot? Some empirical evidence. In P. David and M. Reder (eds.), *Nations and Happiness in Economic Growth: Essays in Honor of Moses Abramowitz*. New York: Academic Press, 89–125.

Easterlin, R., 1995. Will raising the incomes of all increase the happiness of all? *Journal of Economic Behavior and Organization* 27, 35–37.

Easterlin, R. 2001. Income and happiness: Towards a unified theory. *Economic Journal* 111, 465–484.

Ferrer-i-Carbonell, A., and P. Frijters. 2004. How important is methodology for the estimates of the determinants of happiness? *Economic Journal* 114, 641–659.

Ferrer-i-Carbonell, A., and B. M. S. Van Praag. 2002. The subjective costs of health losses due to chronic diseases: An alternative model for monetary appraisal. *Health Economics* 11, 709–722.

Flynn, P., D. Berry, and T. Heintz. 2002. Sustainability and quality of life indicators: Toward the integration of economic, social and environmental measures. *Indicators: The Journal of Social Health* 1(4), 19–39.

Frey, B., and A. Stutzer. 2002. *Happiness and Economics: How the Economy and Institutions Affect Well-Being*. Princeton, NJ: Princeton University Press.

Kahneman, D., P. Wakker, and R. Sarin. 1997. Back to Bentham? Explorations of experienced utility. *Quarterly Journal of Economics* 112, 375–405.

Layard, R. 2005. *Happiness: Lessons from a New Science*. New York: Penguin Press.

Ng, Y. K. 1999. Utility, informed preference, or happiness: Following Harsanyi's argument to its logical conclusion. *Social Choice and Welfare* 16, 197–216.

Ng, Y. K. 2003. From preferences to happiness: Towards a more complete welfare economics. *Social Choice and Welfare* 20, 307–350.

Theories of the Firm

Coase, R. 1937. The nature of the firm. *Econometrica* 4, 386–405.

Cordes, C., P. Richerson, R. McElreath, and P. Strimling. 2008. A naturalistic approach to the theory of the firm: The role of cooperation and cultural evolution. *Journal of Economic Behavior and Organization* 68, 125–139.

Cyert, R., and J. March. 1963. *A Behavioral Theory of the Firm*. Englewood Cliffs, NJ: Prentice-Hall.

Nelson, R., and S. Winter. 1982. *An Evolutionary Theory of the Firm*. Cambridge, MA: Harvard University Press.

Simon, H. 1987. Satisficing. In *New Palgrave Dictionary of Economics*, vol. 4, ed. J. Eatwell, M. Milgate, and P. Newman. London and New York: Macmillan, 243–244.

Wilmhurst, 1978. *The Fundamentals and Practices of Marketing*. London: Heinemann.

Witt, U. 1998. Imagination and leadership—The neglected dimensions of an evolutionary theory of the firm. *Journal of Economic Behavior and Organization* 35, 161–177.

Witt, U. 2005. Firms as realizations of entrepreneurial visons. *Papers on Economics and Evolution* 200510, 1–28.

Other Cited References

Ayres, R. 2008. Sustainability economics: Where do we stand? *Ecological Economics* doi:10.1016/j.ecolecon.207.12.009.

Friedman, M. 1962. *Capitalism and Freedom*. Chicago: University of Chicago Press.

Solow, R. 1974. The economics of resources or the resources of economics. *American Economic Review* 64(2), 1–14.

Zamagni, S. 1995. *The Economics of Altruism*. Aldershot, UK: Edward Elgar.

INDEX

Note: Page numbers followed by *f* indicate figures.

Accounting profit, 63; defined, 76
Ackerman, F., 150, 159
Alchian, Armen, 122
Alleva, E., 131
Altruistic punishment, 121, 129; defined, 137
Anarchy, State, and Utopia (Nozick), 46
Animals, evolution of behavior and, 128–132
Arrow impossibility theorem, 48, 89, 112–114; defined, 55
Ayres, Robert, 167, 169

Barriers to entry, 62
Bayer, H., 134
Behavioral critique, of traditional cost-benefit analysis, 147–150; income and, 147; incommensurability and, 149–150; loss aversion and, 148; losses and gains and social context, 149; psychology of discounting and, 148–149
Behavioral critique, of Walrasian welfare economics, 3, 120–142; empirically established behavioral patterns, 125–128; evolutionary basis of human behavior, 129–132; game theory and, 121–125; importance of correct behavioral assumptions, 135–137; neuroscience and, 132–135
Bentham, Jeremy, 173, 178
Bergson, Abram, 46

Bergsonian social welfare function, 46
Biased cultural transmission, 127; defined, 137
Biodiveristy: ecological value of, 176–177; economic value of, 175–176; loss of, 175; social value of, 176
"Biophilia," 176
Boadway, Robin, 107
Boadway paradox, 107; defined, 116
Bounded rationality, 171; defined, 178
Brekke, Kjell, 109
Bromley, Daniel, 112, 116, 165
Brosnan, S., 129–130
Brouwer's fixed-point theorem, 54–55, 54*f*

Camerer, C., 134
Chipman, J., 109
Clark, J. B., 69
Clark–Wicksteed product exhaustion theorem, 68–69
Cleveland, C., 169
Climate change: economics of, 152–155; limits of Walrasian economics and, 155–156; sustainability and, 150–152, 175
Coase, Ronald, 81, 170
Cobb, Charles, 32
Cobb–Douglas production function, 32–36, 33*f*
Compensating variation, 94, 107; in cost-benefit analysis, 144; defined, 94

Compensation principle. *See* Potential Pareto improvement
Constant elasticity of substitution (CES) function, 34
Constant returns to scale, 34; defined, 40
Constrained bliss point, 46
Constrained optimization: defined, 20; inputs and, 30–31; Lagranian equation, 16–17, 59–60, 72; mathematics of, 14–15
Consumer, neoclassical theory of, 5–23; axioms/assumptions of, 9–10, 11, 12–13; constrained optimization, 16–17; convexity tests, 18–20; discounting, 20, 21*f*; Edgeworth box, 11–13, 11*f*; graphical analysis of barter and trade, 8–11; many Pareto efficiencies, 13–14; mathematical interpretation of utility, 14–15; necessity of independent utilities, 17–18; prices and utility, 58–60, 59*f*; utility theory's foundation, 5–8
Consumer surplus, 86–87, 87*f*; in cost-benefit analysis, 144–145; defined, 94; Hicks and Marshall, 93–94, 93*f*
Contingent valuation method (CVM), 136–137, 143; defined, 137, 159
Continuity, in axioms defining consumer choice, 10
Contractarian approach, to social welfare, 46–47
Contract curve for exchange, 13–14, 14*f*; defined, 20
Contract curve for production, defined, 40
Convexity tests, 18–20; defined, 20–21
Cordes, C., 172
Core of exchange economy, 51, 52*f*; defined, 55
Corporate social responsibility, 172–173; defined, 178
Costanza, R., 176
Cost-benefit analysis, 52, 143–162; behavioral critique of traditional, 147–150; climate change and limits of Walrasian economics, 155–156; consumer surplus and, 94; contemporary experimental economics and, 157–159; defined, 94; efficiency and, 112; potential Pareto improvement and, 102–103; sustainability and economics of climate change, 150–155; welfare economics and foundations of, 143–166
Critical natural capital, 176; defined, 178
Cross-price elasticity, 70–71; defined, 76

Cycling paradox, 104–105, 105*f*; defined, 116
Cyert, R., 172

Deadweight loss, 88; defined, 94
Demand, law of, 62–63, 62*f*, 90; defined, 77, 95
De Martino, B., 133
Derived demand, 66; defined, 76
De Waal, F., 129–130
Diminishing marginal productivity, defined, 40
Diminishing marginal rate of substitution, 10; defined, 21
Diminishing marginal rate of technical substitution, 26–27; defined, 40
Diminishing marginal utility, defined, 21
Diminishing returns, law of, 66; defined, 77
Direct exchange. *See* Consumer, neoclassical theory of
Discounting, 20, 21*f*; defined, 21; economics of climate change and, 153–154; traditional cost-benefit analysis and, 148–149
Dominant strategy: defined, 137; in Prisoner's Dilemma, 122
Dorris, M., 134
Douglas, Paul, 32
Dual, 72, 74–75, 74*f*; defined, 76

Economic actor. *See* Rational actor model
Economic profit, 63; defined, 77
Economics of Climate Change: The Stern Review (Stern), 152–153, 155–156
Economic theory and policy, future of, 163–182; environmental sustainability policies, 175–177; firm as social institution, 170–173; guide for evaluating long-term economic policies, 177–178; laws of thermodynamics and, 166–167; policies for resource base, 167–170; public policy in Walrasian system, 163–166, 164*f*; utility, happiness, and consumers as humans, 173–175
Edgeworth, Francis, 11
Edgeworth box diagram, 168; indifference curves to exchange, 11–13, 11*f*; input allocation, 27–28, 27*f*
Efficiency: ideology of, 111–112, 116; output mix and social welfare, 110–111, 110*f*
Elasticity of consumption: defined, 159; economics of climate change and, 153, 155
Elasticity of substitution, 32–33, 71; in Cobb–Douglas production function, 34–35; defined, 40

Endogenous preferences, 125–128; defined, 137
Endowment effect, 126, 144; defined, 137
Energy return on energy invested (EROEI), 169–170; defined, 178
Engel curve, 92; defined, 95
Entropy law, 166–169; defined, 178, 179
Envelope theorem, 76
Environmental issues. *See* Climate change; Economic theory and policy, future of
Equilibrium. *See* General equilibrium
Equivalent variation, 94, 107; in cost-benefit analysis, 144; defined, 95
EROEI (energy return on energy invested), 169–170; defined, 178
Euler's theorem, 35–36, 68; defined, 40; homogeneity of degree zero, 70–71
Exergy, 169; defined, 178
Existence of equilibrium, 53–55
Exogenous preferences, 135; in axioms defining consumer choice, 10; defined, 21–22, 137
Externalities: defined, 95; market failure and, 80–82, 88

Factor market, 65–68, 66*f*, 67*f*; Clark–Wicksteed product exhaustion theorem, 68–69
Fantino, E., 131
Feldman, A., 113
Firm, as social institution, 170–173
First-order condition for maximizing utility, 60; defined, 77
Fisher, F., 102
Fixed-point theorems, 54–55, 54*f*; defined, 55
Fossil fuel energy, entropy law and, 168–169
Framing effect, 133; defined, 137
Frank, R., 174–175
Frederick, S., 154
Free rider: defined, 138; game theory and, 124; problem of, 88, 129, 165, 171
Frey, B., 174
Friedman, Milton, 115, 117, 165, 171
Function coefficient, 75–76; defined, 77
Future policies. *See* Economic theory and policy, future of

Game theory, economic behavior and, 121–125
General equilibrium, 42–56; assumptions about, 51; defined, 55, 116; existence of equilibrium and, 53–55; Pareto efficiency condition III, 48–51; potential Pareto

improvement, 51–53, 52*f*, 104; production possibilities frontier, 43–45, 45*f*; social welfare function, 46–48, 47*f*; utility possibilities frontier, 42–43, 44*f*
Georgescu-Roegen, Nicholas, 144, 163, 172
Glimcher, P., 131, 134
Global warming. *See* Climate change
Gorman, W. M., 105
Grand utility possibilities frontier (GUPF), 44–46, 45*f*; defined, 55

Habituation, 121, 132; defined, 138
Hall, C., 169
Hanley, N., 136, 157
Hare, B., 128–129
Harper, D., 130
Hartwick–Solow rule, 151; defined, 159
Hedonic pricing, 143; defined, 159
Heinzerling, L., 150, 159
Henrich, J., 123, 125, 129
Hicks, John, 51–52, 90
Hicksian demand curve, 90–93, 91*f*; consumer surplus and, 93–94, 93*f*; defined, 95
Hicksian income: biodiversity and, 175; defined, 116
Homo economicus (economic man). *See* Rational actor model
Homogeneity of degree zero, 70–71
Homogenous function, 35; defined, 40
Homogenous product, in perfect competition, 8
Homothetic utility functions, 100–109, 108*f*; defined, 116
Howarth, Richard, 76
Human behavior. *See* Behavioral critique, of Walrasian welfare economics
Human capital: cost-benefit analysis and, 151, 151*f*; defined, 159
Hyperbolic discounting, 127; defined, 138

Ideology of efficiency, 116
Income: economics of climate change and, 155; traditional cost-benefit analysis and, 147
Income effect, 90–93, 91*f*; defined, 95
Income elasticity, 70–71; defined, 77
Incommensurability problem, 149–150; defined, 159
Inconsistent discounting of future, 121, 127
Independent utilities, necessity of assumption of, 17–18

Indifference curve: defined, 22; Edgeworth box, 11–13, 11*f*; graphical analysis of barter and trade, 8–11, 9*f*; marginal utility, 15
Inferior good, 92; defined, 95
Input exchange. *See* Production, neoclassical theory of
Invisible hand, of market, 7, 57, 69
Isoquant: defined, 40; input allocation, 25–27, 26*f*; mathematical interpretation of, 28–29

Jevons, William Stanley, 1

Kahneman, Daniel, 120, 133, 173
Kaldor, Nicholas, 51–52
Kaldor–Hicks criterion. *See* Potential Pareto improvement
Kaufmann, R., 169
Kuhn–Tucker conditions, 73–74, 73*f*; defined, 77

Lagranian equation, 16–17, 59–60, 72
Lancaster, Kevin, 76
Law of demand, 62–63, 62*f*, 90; defined, 77, 95
Law of diminishing returns, 66; defined, 77
Law of entropy, 166–169; defined, 178, 179
Law of supply, 62–63, 62*f*; defined, 77
Laws of thermodynamics, 166–167; defined, 179
Layard, R., 174
Leontief, Wassily, 31
Leontief/fixed proportion production, 31–32, 32*f*, 33
Lexicographic preferences, 136–137, 150; defined, 138
Linear production function, 31, 31*f*, 33
Lipsey, R. G., 76
Livermore, M., 159
Lockwood, B., 101
Loewenstein, G., 134, 154
Long-run average cost (LRAC) curve, 63–64, 64*f*
Loss aversion, 121, 126, 144; defined, 138, 159; neural basis for, 133; traditional cost-benefit analysis and, 148
Lump-sum transfer, 13; defined, 22; prices and market failure, 88–89

Macroeconomics, microfoundations of, 114–116, 117
Maestripieri, D., 131

Manufactured capital, 151, 151*f*
March, J., 172
Marginal cost of production, 63, 64*f*; production possibilities frontier and, 60–61, 61*f*
Marginal physical product (MPP), 66–67, 67*f*
Marginal product, 28–29; defined, 40
Marginal rate of substitution, 10; defined, 22. *See also* Diminishing marginal rate of substitution
Marginal rate of technical substitution (MRTS), 26; defined, 41. *See also* Diminishing marginal rate of technical substitution
Marginal utility, 15; defined, 22. *See also* Diminishing marginal utility
Marginal utility of money, 60; defined, 77
Market failure, 2–3, 79–96; defined, 95; externalities, 80–82, 88; market power, 85–88, 86*f*, 87*f*; prices and, 88–90; public goods, 82–85, 85*f*, 88
Market power: defined, 95; market failure and, 85–88, 86*f*, 87*f*
Marshall, Alfred, 90
Marshallian demand curve, 90–93, 91*f*; consumer surplus and, 93–94, 93*f*; defined, 95
Melis, A., 128–129
Microfoundations, of macroeconomics, 114–116, 117
Microfoundations project, 38; defined, 41
Monetarism, 115–116; defined, 117
Money illusion, 70; defined, 77
Monopolies, 85–88, 86*f*, 87*f*
Moore, J., 109

Nash, John, 121, 122
Nash Equilibrium, 121–122; defined, 138
Natural capital, 151, 151*f*; defined, 159
Nelson, J., 135
Nelson, R., 172
Neuroeconomics, 132–135; defined, 138
Ng, Y. K., 173
Non-satiation, in axioms defining consumer choice, 9
Nordhaus, W., 153
Normal good, 90; defined, 95
Nozick, Robert, 46–47

O'Donoghue, T., 154
Opportunity cost, 63; defined, 78

Other-regarding behavior, 124–125, 130, 135, 149
Output mix, efficiency and social welfare, 110–111, 110*f*
Own-price elasticity, 70–71; defined, 78

Paradox of voting, 114; defined, 117
Pareto, Vilfredo, 1
Pareto efficiency, 2, 6, 13–14; Condition I, 12, 50; Condition II, 28, 50; Condition III, 48–51, 49*f*; Pareto efficiency in exchange, 22, 41; Pareto efficiency in input allocation, 25, 27–28; proof of perfect competition and, 65. *See also* Potential Pareto improvement
Partial equilibrium: defined, 117; potential Pareto improvement and, 104
Pearce, D., 154
Perfect competition: conditions for, 8; existence of equilibrium and, 53–55; Pareto efficiency and proof of, 65; prices and, 61–64, 62*f*, 64*f*
Perfect elasticity, 66
Perfect information, in perfect competition, 8, 62
Perfect resource mobility, in perfect competition, 8
Pigou, Arthur, 81
Pimentel, David, 168
Pimm, S., 175
Portney, P., 154
Positive economics, 109, 164; defined, 117, 178
Potential Pareto improvement (PPI), 51–53, 52*f*; cost-benefit analysis and, 102–103; defined, 55; public policy and Walrasian economics, 163–164; theoretical paradoxes and, 104–111
Precautionary principle, 148; defined, 160
Preference filtering, 135–137
Preferences: in axioms defining consumer choice, 10; behavioral economics and, 18. *See also* Exogenous preferences
Prelec, D., 134
Price elasticity, 70–71
Prices, 57–78; Clark–Wicksteed product exhaustion theorem, 68–69; constrained optimization, 73–74; dual and function coefficient, 74–76; factor market, 65–68, 66*f*, 67*f*; inputs/outputs/marginal cost, 60–61, 61*f*; Kuhn–Tucker conditions,

73–74, 73*f*; market failure and, 88–90; maximizing utility subject to budget constraint, 58–60, 59*f*; perfect competition, 61–65, 62*f*, 64*f*; theory of the second best, 76; Walrasian economics in practice, 69–72
Price theory, 37
Prisoner's Dilemma, 121–123, 122*f*, 174–175; defined, 138; process-regarding preferences and, 127
Process-regarding preferences, 126–127; defined, 138
Producer surplus, 87*f*, 88; defined, 95
Production, neoclassical theory of, 24–41; assumptions about, 27, 37; constant elasticity of substitution function, 36–37; constrained optimization, 30–31; graphical analysis of input allocation, 25–27; input exchange as foundation of, 24–25; mathematical interpretation of isoquant, 28–29; Pareto efficiency in input allocation, 27–28; prices and, 60–61, 61*f*; production functions, 31–37; separability, 38; Solow Growth Model, 38; Total Factor Productivity, 39–40
Production functions, 25, 39*f*; defined, 41
Production possibilities frontier, 43–45, 45*f*; defined, 55, 78; prices and, 60–61, 61*f*
Prospect theory, 133
Public goods: defined, 95; market failure and, 82–85, 85*f*, 88
Public Goods Game, 121, 124, 128
Public policy. *See* Economic theory and policy, future of
Pure altruism, 121, 128
Pure time preference, 153–154; defined, 160

Quantity equation, 115–116; defined, 117
Quiggin, J., 156

Ramsey, F., 154
Randall, A., 135
Rate of product transformation, 48–51, 49*f*; defined, 55, 78; prices and, 60–61
Rational actor model, 1, 3; Arrow's theorem and interdependency of, 113–114; behavioral assumptions, 9–11, 79–80; defined, 22. *See also* Behavioral critique, of traditional cost-benefit analysis; Behavioral critique, of Walrasian welfare economics

Rawls, John, 47
Real economy, 111; defined, 117
Real income, 90
Regulatory issues, cost-benefit analysis and, 150. *See also* Economic theory and policy, future of
Reinforcing behavior, 132
Revesz, R., 158–159

Samuelson, P., 109
Sarin, R., 173
Satisficing, 171; defined, 178
Schall, J., 134
Schultz, W., 132
Scitovsky, Tibor, 104–105
Second best, theory of the, 76
Second-order condition, 60; defined, 78
Self-interested/self-regarding behavior, 175; exogenous preferences and, 21–22; flaw of Walrasian theory and, 113; game theory and, 123, 125; Second Fundamental Theorem of welfare economics, 89
Separability, 38, 38*f*
Shephard's Lemma, 76
Shogren, J., 157
Simon, Herbert, 171
Slutsky, Eugen, 92
Slutsky equation, 92
Smith, Adam, 7, 57, 69
Social Choice and Individual Values (Arrow), 112
Social price, 80–81; defined, 96
Social welfare function, 46–48, 47*f*, 106; defined, 22, 56; efficiency and output mix, 110–111, 110*f*
Solow, Robert, 38, 167
Solow Growth Model, 38
Spash, C., 136
Stavins, R., 102
Steady-state system, 68
Stern, N., 152–153
Stern Review. See *Economics of Climate Change: The Stern Review*
"Sticking" paradox, 105–107, 106*f*
Stiglitz, Joseph, 101
Strong sustainability, 152, 176; defined, 160
Stutzer, A., 174
Subjective utility, 173; defined, 179
Subjective well-being, 147; defined, 160
Subsidies, as solution to externalities, 81–82

Substitution effect, 90–93, 91*f*; defined, 96
Sunk-cost effect, 128, 131–132; defined, 138
Supply, law of, 62–63, 62*f*; defined, 77
Sustainability, climate change and cost-benefit analysis, 150–152

Taxes, as solution to externalities, 81–82
Taylor's expansion of general production function, 37
Theoretical critique, of Walrasian welfare economics, 101–119; Arrow impossibility theorem, 113, 114; efficiency and, 111–112; importance of, 111; importance of fundamental theorems, 101–103; microfoundations of macroeconomics and, 114–116; potential Pareto improvement and, 104–111; traditional cost-benefit analysis, 143–146
Theory of Justice, A (Rawls), 47
Theory of the second best, 76
Thermodynamics, laws of, 166–167; defined, 179
Thompson, K., 134
Threshold effects, 134; defined, 138
Time inconsistency, 121, 127; defined, 138
Tom, S., 133
Tomasello, M., 128–129
Topology, 54. *See also* Fixed-point theorems
Total differentiation, 15
Total factor productivity, 36, 39–40, 71–72, 169; defined, 41
Tragedy of the commons, 83
Transitivity, in axioms defining consumer choice, 10, 105
Translog function, 37
Tversky, A., 133

Ultimatum Game, 121, 122–124; defined, 139; process-regarding preferences and, 126–127
Utility: defined, 22; foundations of theory, 5–8; mathematical interpretation of, 14–15; maximizing subject to budget constraint, 58–60, 59*f*
Utility function, defined, 22
Utility possibilities frontier, 42–43, 44*f*; defined, 56

Veblen, Thorstein, 120
Velocity of money, 115; defined, 117

Wagner, A., 102
Wagner, G., 102
Wakker, P., 173
Walras, Léon, 1, 24, 170
Walrasian economics, 1–2; assumptions
    of, 79–80; in practice, 69–72; summary
    of, 103; three building blocks of, 2–3;
    traditional cost-benefit analysis and,
    143–146. *See also* Behavioral critique,
    of traditional cost-benefit analysis;
    Behavioral critique, of Walrasian welfare
    economics; Theoretical critique, of
    Walrasian welfare economics; Welfare
    economics
Warr, D., 169
Weak sustainability, 150–151, 151*f*, 175;
    defined, 160
Weitzman, Martin, 156

Welfare benefits of trade, 2
Welfare economics, 1; defined, 23; First
    Fundamental Theorem of, 2, 65, 89–90,
    101, 103; Second Fundamental Theorem of,
    2–3, 88–90, 101–102; Third Fundamental
    Theorem of, 89. *See also* Walrasian
    economics
Weyant, J., 154
Wicksteed, Phillip, 69
Williams, John, 122
Willingness to accept compensation (WTA),
    93
Willing to pay for gain (WTP), 93
Wilson, E. O., 176
Winter, S., 172
Witt, U., 172

Zamagni, S., 173, 175

The authorized representative in the EU for product safety and compliance is:
Mare Nostrum Group
B.V Doelen 72
4831 GR Breda
The Netherlands

www.ingramcontent.com/pod-product-compliance
Lightning Source LLC
Chambersburg PA
CBHW062027270326
41929CB00014B/2352